THE ART OF
HUNTING HUMANS

A radical and confronting explanation of the human mind

SIDNEY MAZZI

ISBN: 1-7919-6075-8
ISBN-13: 978-1-7919-6075-9

NOTICE

The Art of Hunting Humans presents key aspects of the human mind. With straightforward language, weird metaphors and practical examples, it enables readers to understand human behaviour and **evaluate their lives from an outsider's perspective**.

Designed to **CHALLENGE** rather than comfort, *The Art of Hunting Humans* sets itself apart from anything else written in its field. The result is a sceptical, radical explanation of the mind that provides extraordinary insights into the inner worlds of human beings.

Note from the author

I don't want to risk giving away too much from start — I've never liked spoilers. Hence, I've not included a preface for this book. You'll just have to jump right in. However, if at any time you feel that I'm teasing too much, don't give up. Instead, visit **HuntingHumans.com** and read my short series of articles, *Chasing Greatness*. You will get a better sense of what I am trying to achieve. The articles should also alleviate any reservations you may hold about my unorthodox writing approach. Hopefully, armed with a bit of context, you will then enjoy reading this book.

The articles:

Chasing Greatness I – The Return of the forgotten Virtue
A dream or a manifesto. I am not sure. You tell me.

Chasing Greatness II – The Diamond of Wisdom
A symbol (and a tool) to guide your journey

Chasing Greatness III – Reasons for my approach
Some of you won't like this article, but I can't please everyone and remain authentic

Chasing Greatness IV – The key detail that even Elon Musk missed
First, we need to become "the tribe of the wise"

HuntingHumans.com

CONTENTS

1
INTRODUCTION
EXPLORING HUMAN IGNORANCE & FLAWS

Nothing compares to the thrill of chasing the perfect prey. Hunting socially sophisticated primates, known as human beings, is the ultimate mission any creature can pursue — the most challenging and fascinating journey one can take. In this book, written by experienced hunters, we explore key aspects of human behaviour. We also provide practical tips for how to use — to your advantage — the ignorance that humans display about their nature.

Human beings are planet Earth's smartest and most dangerous animals. With superior intelligence, there is no doubt that they are formidable — far more difficult to ensnare than the lesser of Earth's creatures, such as lions or bears. However, if you have the fortitude to complete this book, you will join a select club of hunters who have the ability to exploit human behaviour to their advantage.

BEYOND BIG-GAME HUNTING

Big-game hunting is the pursuit of large animals, such as lions and elephants. Though not the largest of Earth's creatures, humans present many challenges, even for the most seasoned hunters. Have you ever observed humans in their natural habitat? If so, you might have noticed that their behaviour is more challenging to identify and predict than regular large terrestrial mammals. Due to the complex human central-intelligence system, human behaviour is more sophisticated than that of all other Earth-born creatures. Never forget, though, that these 'smart monkeys' are animals, nonetheless, with instincts and patterns of behaviour that you can exploit.

It is important to know that some humans are territorial, just like we see with gorillas and kangaroos. Believe it or not, lots of them still think that there is a need for a chest-beating alpha male within their group. Should you step into their territory without putting some measures in place, beware; these humans can be very dangerous. Yes, territorial humans can be violent, but, at the same time, they are the easiest to trap.

Interestingly, some humans use sex to gain social acceptance and protection, just as we observe in chimps. Then there are, of course, others with needs and wants that are less apparent. What matters for now is that there are several different types of humans, and some can also be tribal and highly prone to delusion. So, you need to keep in mind that to hunt a human, you must know what type you have in your sights. Then, you will possess the necessary knowledge to select the tastiest bait.

In a nutshell, if you understand how to play with a human's desires, he should not be a difficult catch. In general, these creatures are also disinclined to engage in rational analysis, even though very few of them are aware of the fact. So, after reading this book, we hope you will be able to observe these characteristics easily and understand how most humans, even their leaders, continually embarrass themselves with weak behaviours that are plain to see.

SOME OF THE WEAKNESSES WE WILL EXPLORE

When hunting humans, there are many weaknesses you can exploit. Here are two:

<u>Just like dogs</u>
A fundamental feature to play with is the trust that humans have in their emotions, feelings, sensations — or whatever you want to call those things. This trust provides a big opportunity.

Why? Well, because humans don't realise that their brains train them like a human would train a dog. Instead of a tasty treat or clip around the ear, though, the brain uses good or bad emotions to train a human to do what it believes he should. So, we will teach you how to mislead a human's brain into sending emotions that will cause your prey to 'choose' to do what you want.

For almost every human, it's hard to see that this manipulation is happening; their understanding of which rewards a human brain recognises is too narrow. For example, for most humans, any act carried out for anything other than money, recognition or acceptance is usually seen as an act for no reward. Humans have a weak understanding of the multiple kinds of rewards their brains might seek. So, when used well, even minimal external stimuli can do the trick. We will show you how to exploit this.

Fear is gold

To manipulate a human, you can intimidate him by using fear, or you can enthral him by playing with his vanity. We will go deeply into both, but we can tell you in advance that, of the two tactics, intimidation is the simplest and most effective — especially as most humans behave like cornered, starving beasts that see everything as a possible threat. It's also usually more fun playing with a human's fear than his vanity.

As you probably can imagine, this reality again stems from the dreadful understanding humans have of the workings of their minds and bodies. In this book, we uncover the roots of human anger and hatred, and you will learn to manipulate these feelings. To play with them successfully with your chosen prey, though, you must understand (better than it) the origin and complexity of a human's emotions. You must know, too, why he feels and reacts the way he does.

Finally, we will present several other flaws to explore. A human's need for social approval is one of the easiest to manipulate. His misunderstanding of the meaning of uncertainty is also important. It all depends on the type of hunter you are. What do you enjoy the most, to seduce or terrify?

IGNORANCE IS WIDESPREAD

There is no need to rush. Take your time to learn all the tricks and practise them. Humans will not uncover this knowledge any time soon, and we will tell you why.

First, almost all books designed to help humans understand themselves are a joke — we recently cracked their codes of communication and read some of these books. What we found is priceless. These books do offer some interesting insights. The problem, though, is that in almost all cases, they are either designed for 'losers', or they are too damned technical. Not surprisingly, even the smartest humans don't usually read these 'tomes of wisdom'.

Secondly, for humans, discussing human behaviour with each other is usually problematic; more often than not, the discussion is tangled with religion, superstition and supernatural fantasies. So, for humans, spreading knowledge about how their species behaves is almost impossible, which, on a positive note, makes your life easier.

Thirdly, humans are often deeply emotionally invested in preserving their ignorance of unsettling truths.

So, most victims you will play with, even highly educated leaders, won't have a clue about what makes humans 'tick'. Among humans, ignorance is widespread. As a consequence, even today, humans still embarrass themselves by doing obvious things that they could easily avoid. Throughout this book, we expose and explore these embarrassments.

KNOW YOUR PREY

Finally, Sun Tzu, one of Earth's most famous practitioners of war, once said: *"Know the enemy and know yourself; in a hundred battles you will never be in peril."* Let's repeat the most important part for this book: *'Know the enemy'*. This is the key. You must take the time to observe your prey and know it better than it does. In fact, once you finish this book, you will be able to understand humans better than themselves. Then, you will be able to manipulate your prey; 'pull its strings', like a master puppeteer. We will show you how. Enjoy!

2

ROADMAP & WARNINGS

A GUIDE TO THIS BOOK

Over the following chapters, we will explore human behaviour from an alternative point of view. It is essential that you alter how you view human beings. YOU MUST make something of a paradigm shift, which can be harder than you think. Forget everything you know about humans and start from scratch. To help you to change your mindset and attitude, we will start with some basic concepts.

THE GUIDE

<u>Part I – WARM UP – THE ISOLATED CAPTAIN</u>: To warm up (or sharpen your blade) we will discuss two very basic ideas. First we will quickly pass by the human communication system — which humans trust implicitly, and that's a mistake. Secondly, we will expose how (and from where) humans perceive reality. You will start to see the difference between seeing and projecting reality, which is crucial for understanding your prey.

Interestingly, this understanding will allow us, for example, to demonstrate why humans are condemned to repeat the same mistakes time and time again.

5

Note again that the ideas we present here are basic, but crucial — a necessary foundation for you to build upon your understanding of the human animal. Having this solid foundation will pay off. Additionally, the whole thing will get more complicated as we move towards the end. Wait and see.

Part II – <u>DIGGING DEEPER INTO YOUR PREY'S REALITY</u>: To get a firm understanding of humans' inner worlds, we dig into their reality — an essential theme of this book that permeates all parts. You will begin to see why warming up (sharpening your blade) was necessary.

Part III – <u>BETWEEN REALITIES & DESIRES</u>: After exposing the chaos that is humans' perceived reality, we demonstrate how it spurs them on to act, one way or another, by delving into the roles of emotions and desires.

Part IV – <u>WHAT DRIVES THE ANIMAL</u>: You will learn to play with what drives humans: fear and vanity — all while appealing to your quarry's self-interest. You will also see topics like *How to choose your bait*. Yes, here you will start to become the master puppeteer.

Part V – <u>SECRETS BEHIND HUMAN IGNORANCE</u>: Step by step, we demonstrate why humans are so clueless. You will discover that they build cages and feed internal 'enemies', that their lack of self-understanding plays into the hands of us hunters, and why it is nearly impossible for humans to spend time fixing their problems. We reveal secrets to control the enemies humans harbour within.

Part VI – <u>SUPERIORS</u>: Here you meet the *SUPERIORS* — creatures like no other. You'd better be ready!

ADDITIONAL NOTES

<u>It is NOT a complete mystery:</u> Note that few of the features discussed will come as a complete surprise to humans. Many will have heard about them at some point in their lives. However, it is only when you clearly

understand these features and put THEM ALL together, while in the right frame of mind, that you will make a difference. It takes practice, though.

<u>Sometimes written like a summary</u>: It is important to note that we will pass over some parts quickly — summarise — because, as explained, a few concepts are basic — like the one in the following chapter — and, whenever we can, we aim to tackle more complex topics.

<u>A wide range of examples</u>: We also must warn you that we use many examples. After all, for you to understand human nature thoroughly, we must detail human characteristics and, at times, REPEAT ourselves using examples to explain our point adequately. Otherwise, how could you possibly understand why some humans who are about to speak in public, with heart pounding, feel like a gladiator ready to fight in the Coliseum? Or, how could you know that a simple conversation about who washes the dishes could be a proxy for the feeling of acceptance called "love"? Weird, don't you think? So, we will be rather didactic. After all, we're here to teach the craft of human hunting, not to entertain you.

<u>"Tell a human this story:"</u> As you know, humans are more complicated than other Earth-born creatures. Therefore, to explain their features and behaviours, we make comparisons to other animals and apply a range of, sometimes weird, metaphors. We show examples from a human's perspective through illustrations called *<u>"Tell a human this story,"</u>* which show how skewed humans' understanding of reality is. These illustrations will help you comprehend human behaviour and solidify the knowledge you've learned. Our illustrations will always be followed by a more practical explanation called, *<u>"How does this apply to humans? And how can you use it against them?"</u>*

<u>No! It's NOT just hunting experience</u>: As a final note for this book, humans' minds are so grotesque that there will be moments when you might question whether we are talking from real hunting experience, or just putting forth wild theories. Well, indeed, we have decades of experience hunting humans, which has helped a lot, but the knowledge

we share is based on more than experience — human 'mind specialists', too, hold similar knowledge.

<u>Don't believe us blindly. Whenever you read something you struggle to accept, test it.</u> Yes! Try it out on a human. After all, you must surely have a pet human or know someone who does! And, don't worry: Tell the pet's owner that you're conducting a mind-and-behaviour test, and it won't hurt a bit.

THE ODDS ARE AGAINST YOU

It's also important to highlight that we aim to accomplish a task that no human has yet achieved: To explain how the human mind works on a large scale. Don't underestimate the challenge.

You are welcome to quit this book at any time. Why not now? Do it! It's probably not for you anyway. We encourage you to leave.

Yes, we designed this book for large-scale reach (in the tens of thousands), but, still, in our experience, just a tiny fraction of readers will have the necessary qualities to understand it fully. Hence, the chances that you have what it takes are slim.

So, as said at the start, you need fortitude to complete this book. It's not for all, and we don't intend it to be.

PART I
WARM UP
THE ISOLATED CAPTAIN

3
JUST CODES
A BROKEN COMMUNICATION SYSTEM

If we fully understand how inefficiently humans communicate with one another, we can use this knowledge against them.

To show you how important this is, during wars, one side will often target its opponent's communication channels to isolate, divide and mislead. So, when hunting, understanding the intricacies of your prey's communication is vital.

As you know, many of Earth's animals communicate through sounds and gestures. Humans, however, use more complex sets of codes and symbols that seem efficient, which is the inaccurate perception we will explore.

Let's first start with a weird metaphor that exaggerates the problem.

<u>Tell a human this story: Flags & smoke signals</u>

Imagine an ancient sailing ship with a bank of oars, several cannons and hundreds of crew. To communicate with other vessels, the captain uses several flags to send coded messages (stating the country his ship comes from, its purpose, if it is a merchant or warship, etc.), which receivers then decipher using a codebook.

Or, picture villages that are miles apart communicating using smoke signals.

<u>How does this apply to humans? And how can you use it against them?</u>
Now, no human would expect recipients of the messages to understand all that is happening on the other end. How could they? And, humans know full well that using a set of codes, such as flags or smoke signals, to communicate would be extremely limiting. This is obvious. For some reason, though, humans struggle to understand that their everyday language, too, is inefficient; it is just a system of codes and symbols that are ripe for misinterpretation.

WORDS, FLAGS & SMOKE SIGNALS
ALL ARE JUST INEFFICIENT SETS OF CODES

Ask a human to speak a foreign language (that he knows quite well, but it is not his native tongue) to explain what's going on within his head, and he will soon realise how cumbersome his words are for speaking his mind. It's easy to see that he would feel limited in his capacity to express himself. And, he wouldn't be at all surprised, either; after all, it's not his first language! What humans don't realise, though, is that even the words they grew up with are clumsy vehicles for self-expression — just a set of codes.

Language is merely a translation into words of the images inside a human's head. However, because communicating in one's 'mother tongue' feels natural, humans have a hard time accepting that words are vague facsimiles of what they want to express. Humans often think that they are explaining themselves completely because it feels natural — they are accustomed to the code.

Let's be very clear. If a human states something simple, like "I want an apple," obviously the other human will understand. What we are saying, though, is that the imagined apple could have a slightly different shape, colour and size to what the receiver understands. You see, *apple* is just a word representing a thought. The gaps between meaning and interpretation become bigger when humans discuss topics that are subjective, like hierarchy, power, money, relationships, expectations and success. It is the bigger gaps that we want to explore.

As if the inefficiency of human language isn't enough, humans filter these codes and symbols depending on factors such as their past experiences, mood, insecurities and knowledge (but this is a topic for a later chapter). What matters for now is that misunderstandings can become much worse because, as you will see, in complex situations a code can have multiple meanings.

CONCLUSIONS

The codes humans use to communicate are highly inefficient, like old submarines that transmit Morse code to each other. Of course, one craft won't be able to express everything that is happening inside its shell. So, in the same way, no human can express himself fully, even though they all like to think they can. So, when humans filter rough codes from other humans, it's easy to understand why there is so much confusion on planet Earth.

For you, knowing this simple truth about the inefficiency of humans' sets of codes is valuable. Wait and see. You can use it to your advantage in situations where misunderstandings take place, and even create misunderstanding for your benefit.

In the next chapter, we show how each animal creates its own reality. By exposing how humans perceive (and distort) the world around them, we will start to demonstrate how isolated within themselves they are and how their codes give away tips for how to manipulate them.

4
ALTERNATIVE REALITIES
INSIDE THE CABIN

Let's look at another example. And, yes, we'll stick with the captain and ship examples — it's essential that you have a solid and natural understanding of the separation between a human's Captain (consciousness) and his Crew.

<u>Tell a human this story: The Captain inside his Cabin</u>

Again, imagine the ancient sailing ship described in the previous chapter. The captain, due to his importance and desire to avoid possible attacks, spends his days working in isolation inside his cabin.

Of course, the captain needs to know what's happening on and around his ship — he's in charge, after all — and, when necessary, he relies on messengers to keep him informed. And inform him they do; although, it's important to understand the limitations of the messages they deliver.

So, here is the sequence: First the lookout sees something. Then, he explains his sighting to the messenger, who then explains to the captain. Simple. Now, consider this:

A lookout, perched high in the ship's crow's nest, spies an approaching vessel. Now, this lookout's knowledge of ships is minimal — he's young and has been a sailor for only a few weeks. Consequently, he can't distinguish between an ancient frigate, caravel or galley — they all look the same to him.

If this young lookout knew more, he would probably notice features such as the number of sails, oars or cannons the ship has. But, to discern and describe those features, and the difference between the vessels, first requires a basic understanding of ships.

It's not surprising that when the young lookout reports his sighting to a messenger below, he can't explain the details very well — he hasn't noticed them. The lookout makes 'best guesses' about the object he has seen based on what he knows and his past experiences.

When the messenger eventually reports news of the approaching ship to the captain, can you understand how compromised the message might be? In the same way, the description of the surroundings will also be compromised because the lookout will never be able to explain precisely the shape of the clouds, the waves, the wind. He will just state general weather conditions, without significant details, unless the captain really pushes him.

You see, the integrity of a message depends on what the lookout saw (or didn't see) — the amount of information he can translate into words compared to the picture he sees — and his ability to explain his sighting to the messenger. And finally, how the messenger then explains it to the captain.

<u>How does this apply to humans? And how can you use it against them?</u>
What humans don't realise is that when their central system (brain) receives information (from eyes and ears), like the lookout and messenger, it makes 'best guesses' about what the information means and what to send to their Captain.

As expected, not all best guesses or translations are the same. In fact, they are slightly different. So, what a human sees and notices is slightly different to the others around him. This is because what a human sees, hears or smells isn't reality; instead, it is a hugely filtered best guess of what is real. Consequently, every human being's interpretation of reality is different. It is interpreted and replayed inside his head, like a hallucination. This may all sound crazy, but you will get what we mean.

You will also learn how different points of view change how you observe human behaviour.

For example, if a human knows about fashion, he will notice subtle nuances between items of dress — the material, the thread — that others will not — 'non-followers of fashion' will literally see no differences between the clothes. Each human's brain projects different images inside his head. The same applies to those knowledgeable in pretty much anything, like types of cars and houses. As weird as it sounds, images, sounds or tastes don't reach the Captain as you might think. He literally sees (or hallucinates) a standard item of clothing without the details. If, however, you ask him to pay attention and check it out again while you explain the differences, details will emerge that he will swear were not there before. The same thing happens with new car designs; one human will see the latest trend in shape, and the other will be oblivious to it unless it is pointed out and explained. It is not just attention differences; every human's Captain sees different images.

The same applies to taste. Take beer (or wine, or even tea) for example. Humans will each experience diverse sensations, depending on how much they know and care about beer. Just like the captain must train his lookout and messenger to differentiate types of ships, so they can provide more accurate information, humans also must undergo a lengthy training process to sharpen their sensitivity to develop the ability to differentiate between types of beer. So, as mentioned before, attention plays a significant role here, but it is not just that. The ability of humans to distinguish between types of beer, dresses or cars will vary between them, and if a human's Lookout doesn't translate accurately, he literally sees just a beer, or a dress or, like in the story above, a ship. His brain (Messenger) decodes the message in a standard, rudimentary way.

So, two humans in the same room seeing and tasting the same things actually have different experiences, depending on their knowledge, culture and past — as well as some other stuff. Each human lives in a different reality because their brain translates information from their senses differently. Of course, this feature doesn't make much difference in simple situations, like two humans seeing the same apple. However, it gets interesting when things become complicated — and they always do. As you will see in Part II, these differences can expand in unbelievable ways, and you can use them while in pursuit of your prey.

A human hears a song in an unfamiliar language. If he learns the lyrics, next time he listens, the music will affect him differently. The first time will be a blur; second time around, though, the human will listen to the words — the music will seem different. It is like a musician who hears songs differently to non-musical humans. In his mind, he can clearly separate the sound of each instrument or notice mistakes made by performers. So, a musician and a non-musician will hear different music. It is not just attention, but their brains translate the music differently. In effect, what they are listening to is different.

<u>Note:</u> The idea is not (or should not be) new to humans. Take touch for example: Humans are well aware that those who are blind can usually detect tactile information faster and in more detail than seeing humans because the brain of a blind human is better trained to collect information from touch. However, very few humans realise that the same beer he and his allies drink together tastes different to each of them.

DIFFERENT REALITIES CAN EXPAND TO SITUATIONS

Differing realities don't only apply to objects or tastes, but experiences and situations, too. Tell a human that in a movie, before the adventure starts, there are usually two events. One is a hook, an opening scene to grab the viewer's attention, which often evokes an immediate emotion, piques curiosity, or is funny, suspenseful or scary. In the second event, the protagonist usually can be seen laughing with or missing his family (maybe looking at an old picture). The viewer may also see him making a cute mistake or revealing a weakness. What's the point of all this? Well, it enables the audience to connect and engage with and care about the protagonist, to feel like he is one of them. So, once a human knows all this, he will start noticing a pattern in the next movies he sees.

If a human reads about basic sales techniques, he will notice when they are applied to him. The same happens if he learns about a sport's tactics and strategies and then watches a game. So, if simple information can change how humans perceive a movie, sales transaction or sporting match, can you imagine how differently they can perceive other situations in life?

THE WORLD OUTSIDE IS TOO COMPLICATED, SO HUMANS WORK WITH LIMITED INFORMATION

In truth, when humans know or care about something, they see more. The volume of information humans continuously gather from their sensors is enormous. So, inside the human head, there is no way the Messenger can inform the Captain of everything. And so, humans see more of what they know or what they want. For example, a pregnant woman is cognizant of other expecting mothers. A criminal spies police around every corner.

As a result, the brain doesn't inform a human of everything; it chooses what to report and the amount of detail. If you don't believe us, ask a neuroscientist on Earth. Because the ratio is so staggeringly low — most information captured is simply ignored — we prefer not to mention it here due to the risk of discrediting our book .

In fact, the brain is pretty good at NOT informing its Captain. This is also true in simple situations. For example, if a human sat down to read this book, he wouldn't feel his butt on his chair until he read this sentence.

As well as ignoring parts of reality, the brain can also mislead the human by providing incorrect information when its best guess is inaccurate.

So, if a human who suffers from arachnophobia sees something resembling a spider, his brain might place an image of a real eight-legged 'terror' in his mind and send him into a mad panic. In such a situation, for a brief moment, the human really does see a spider! Yes, we know it's that crazy.

Note: Here, again, it is important to highlight that the idea that humans ignore facts and are incapable of seeing reality is not entirely new to these animals. For example, humans are well aware that during a stage, which they call "being in love", a love-struck human often alters his reality and, so, is unable to spot defects in his partner (or he simply minimises their importance). So, humans are sort of aware of this phenomena. However, what they fail to acknowledge, and where an opportunity arises for us, is that humans distort reality continuously and at much deeper levels than they think.

<u>A trained eye matters:</u>

Interestingly, how well-trained a human's brain is at seeing something alters how they see it.

Here's a simple example: Humans from one part of the world generally struggle to differentiate between humans from another. To illustrate this point, humans from a place on Earth called Europe may be unable to distinguish between two dark-haired humans from Asia (another place on Earth) who generally feature facial characteristics unique to Asians. Of course, there are exceptions. But, let's say that, in general, a brain from Europe is likely to be less adept at noticing details in an Asian face than a brain raised in Asia. And, it works both ways: Many Asians find it tough differentiating between two blonde-haired Europeans. Of course, this example is also valid in many other parts of the world and situations.

Remember, every day a human is exposed to an avalanche of information, and only a fraction will reach his awareness (the Captain). This is because his 'capable' Messenger has the Captain all figured out and removes what he thinks is irrelevant. Believe it or not, humans don't realise that this filtering takes place, which is unfortunate for them and lucky for you. They are like a naive ship's captain who believes that the lookout and the messenger are telling him everything (every detail) that is happening around the ship.

THE POWER OF THE MESSENGER

In the case described at the beginning of this chapter, with the captain always inside the cabin, humans will understand that the captain relies heavily on the lookout and messenger to decide which information is relevant and, therefore, what to tell him. The captain must trust their capacity to understand and describe what's going on and question them whenever necessary.

With all that we have said, it is critical to note how important the role of the Messenger (the brain) is. As you have just read, he is the one who explains information to the Captain. Based on culture, knowledge and experience, the Messenger decides what the Captain should be aware of (or not) and how the message should get to him.

And, if you think about it, you will realise the enormous influence the

Messenger has; he controls which information the Captain receives, and he chooses how it's delivered. In effect, the Messenger can adjust the narrative to influence the Captain's decision. And one of the crucial elements of a great deception is to convince your victim that he is in control.

Meanwhile, the daily life of a human is complicated, and it is impossible to pay attention to everything. So, he will usually see whatever truth he wants and even have arguments to support it.

Shall we complicate things even more? Yes, let's. A human's reality isn't shaped by just culture, knowledge or experiences. He also sees things differently depending on his mood. The Messenger chooses what a human pays attention to and how it is presented, depending on whether he is happy, sad, confident or scared. Very strange. A human's perception depends not only on his mood but also on the hormones he produces (or lacks) as well as the substances he consumes. All these factors play a role, and the Messenger has a big influence.

For some of you, it may sound simple and obvious, but this information will be valuable when things get more complicated. Hold your horses; we are just warming up.

THE CAPTAIN IS ALWAYS INSIDE THE CABIN
Always

The key thing to understand is that every human sees the world from inside his head — the Captain's Cabin. Everything is a replication of what is going on outside.

Basically, humans live in a constant hallucination — like they are wearing virtual-reality goggles. This idea is a fundamental shift from thinking that images come directly from outside and will enable you to understand that what each human animal sees can be a different translation of what is actually happening around them.

When a human touches another human's hand, what he feels is his brain's translation of the sensation, not the hand's. All emotions and sensations are translations of what is happening outside the human's body. Yes, it sounds obvious and strange all at once, but there is a gaping chasm between the two understandings. We will refer to this fact throughout the book because, in the end, it's the emotions inside their heads that matter to humans. You can replicate these emotions to enthral your prey and lead it into whatever trap you set.

***

The previous paragraph is critical for understanding this book, so read it again.
***

If a human loves something (another person or a status symbol, like a luxury car), it's not actually the thing or object he loves; instead, it's the sensation that the object gives him. This may sound like we are playing with words and definitions (we did warn you), but we're not. We're just explaining a different mindset. So, with this rationale, if you can manipulate sensations that humans love by replicating them inside their heads, you will have the power to shape them without needing the object.

And how can you do this? Well, you must understand why your prey's brain rewards him with some sensations, and punishes him with others.

As the hunter, you must understand what the object means, what need it fulfils. And, you will see this meaning isn't so obvious.

This is important. While many things can hurt a human, they are limited by reality. The number of possible dangers, however, that a human is afraid of is several times greater because of the magnifying power of his imagination.

TAKEAWAYS FROM THIS CHAPTER

Everything happens inside out, like an in-built projector. If you understand the difference between seeing and projecting the stuff around you, you should find this book, and humans, easy to understand.

The misunderstandings about reality that we have mentioned seem small, but, as you will see, they add up.

Before we jump to the next chapter, let's look at how humans use blame and denial to alter their reality.

BONUS
THE INNER FAKE-NEWS GENERATOR

Blame and denial are often used to distort a human's perception, so he can cope with reality. Both features are easy to observe and understand once you look at humans with the right perspective.

But, first, check out this example.

<u>Tell a human this story: The Weak Captain</u>
Again, imagine the same sailing ship. Now, while navigating freezing waters, the vessel hits an iceberg that punctures a hole in its hull.

Consider the fact that on this ship the captain is known to lose his temper and blame others; in other words, he is perceived as a weak leader.

A weak or overly emotional captain will be of little use for solving the problem of a damaged ship, so the messenger tries to protect the status quo and avoid more problems by telling the captain an untruth. Yes, instead of explaining that the hole is the result of a lookout's failure to notice the iceberg, the messenger claims that another vessel is responsible.

In other words, the messenger says whatever necessary to avoid the additional headache an overly emotional captain is bound to create.

Needless to say, no one will address the issue of why the lookout failed to spot the iceberg, and there is a good chance that the ship will have another collision in the future.

<u>How does this apply to humans? And how can you use it against them?</u>
The message contained in the above example would be obvious to almost any human. Strangely, though, when it comes to their lives, they have a hard time recognising good leadership. For many, 'ranting and raving' and refusing to accept blame is often a sign of strength — of being a tough leader. No, we're not joking.

What we're saying may sound stupid, but this is how the minds of many humans work.

If a human is weak and in a situation he can't cope with, he will often say things like *"It did not happen,"* and *"They are to blame,"* and he will BELIEVE what he says is true. You see, for a human being, his perception of reality is often uncomfortable, so his ever-vigilant brain suppresses and alters reality to protect his fragile Captain. Yes, the Messenger tricks the Weak Captain to avoid additional problems.

The Weak Captain is not only present in a few humans, as you might be thinking, but in the vast majority. To expose the depth of the problem, we will share what we recently observed, not just with a regular run-of-the-mill human, but with one of their world's most powerful leaders, known by many as "Mr Orange". Recently, this world leader blamed one of his actions on an advisor. To repeat, it was Mr Orange's action, not his advisor's; however, he publicly blamed his subordinate. You see, Mr Orange thought he was protecting himself by laying blame. Actually, to experienced hunters, he revealed himself as a weak leader who can't filter advice and choose the right people. Why so? Well, it should be obvious that he is responsible for his decisions (he is the leader, isn't he?) and for choosing whom should advise him. And, most importantly, Mr Orange showed the world that he can't cope with the consequences of his actions.

So, needing to blame others is usually a sign of weakness and very few humans are fully aware of the fact. While on Earth, you will often see humans attempt to protect themselves in this way, even though doing so should be embarrassing.

Note: Obviously some humans who lay blame are simply lying. But, they're not whom we are discussing here. In many cases, humans steadfastly BELIEVE what they say — they're not faking. Like the ship's messenger, their brains create alternative information to protect the status quo. As bizarre as it sounds, in lots of cases, these humans truly believe they are right. This idea of humans creating alternative realities isn't easy to accept, but it will make it much easier for you to understand the curious and abnormal behaviour of your prey.

As you will observe, a large portion of humans are immune to reason and facts, and it is not unusual for them to deny problems exist if they don't like the consequences. And, if a human wishes to change another human's mind, providing more information to support an argument won't help. The human will usually ignore what he hears, and his Messenger will tell his Captain a different, more palatable, story. It's as simple as that.

For example, a human reads a health expert's recommendations for the daily consumption of proteins, carbohydrates, vitamins, calories, alcohol and caffeine — even the number of hours to exercise or work. The human will usually agree with what he can comply with and question what he can't. He will say something like, *"Nice research. I agree that we shouldn't eat that much, but, come on! This limit for alcohol is way too low. There are loads of new studies about alcohol, and we can't trust them completely."* And the same happens if the difficult part to comply with is exercise, the amount of eggs to eat per day, etc. As odd as it sounds, humans usually believe what they are saying.

You can see a lot of this when humans discuss politics — good things about 'bad' candidates and bad things from 'good' candidates are simply denied. It's fun to watch.

***

As a rule of thumb, if your human prey doesn't like the outcome of something, he will usually question the problem and deny it existed in the first place. This way he doesn't have to deal with the consequences. Often, his denial will be at the Messenger's, not the Captain's, level. So, he'll truly believe in what he says. We kid you not!

***

<u>Tip:</u> If you observe that your chosen human prey frequently presents symptoms similar to the Weak Captain, he is probably easy to catch. Don't rush. Take your time. You can agree with him and deny a problem, help him create an enemy to blame, or reinforce the blame he has placed on another human or object. Doing this will usually bring the human relief and he will link your presence to pleasure, which will make him easy to enthral later.

***

But, remember, don't ever offer solutions for the problem your prey complains about; if you do, it won't help you manipulate him. In these cases, humans are usually immune to reason and don't want a solution; they'd prefer to lay blame and express their criticisms and disappointments. If you offer a solution, you will secretly remove a human's excuse to 'belly ache'. He will most likely hate you, which will destroy a bond of confidence that you would have been able to explore later. So, don't offer solutions!

When you see a human in denial or blaming others, don't interrupt. Remember this quote by one of Earth's greatest warmongers:

***

"Never interrupt your enemy when he is making a mistake" —
Napoleon Bonaparte.
***

Of course, there are times when someone else is the root of a human's misfortune. However, those occasions are rare, and if a human digs deep enough he will often realise that at least some of the blame rests squarely on his shoulders. For example, when a human complains about his partner (too picky, or jealous, or insecure) he should bear in mind that it was he who chose the partner in the first place.

So, while hunting, always keep in mind that when humans deny or blame, it is usually a sign of weakness and immaturity. In most cases, they truly believe they are right. They are immune to reality. So, listen to a human who often blames something else. He'll reveal plenty of clues and be easy to catch.

5

THE ISOLATED CAPTAIN
FIRST TIPS

By now, we're sure you are itching to hunt some human! They sound like fascinating prey, wouldn't you say? However, which bait do you plan to use? Remember, every human processes information differently, so one 'flavour' most certainly does not fit all. To understand which bait is best for your chosen prey, you must first study the mechanics of the human mind. It will take time to learn the complexities and all the different types but, first, we want to give you a glimpse of some things you can conclude by looking at humans from the Captain's perspective. What you are about to see is a BASIC example — we're preparing the foundations for major conclusions that we'll reveal later.

The first practical application
REPETITION

With the Captain-in-the-cabin mindset, it is easy to understand why humans are usually condemned, fated — cursed — to repeat the same mistakes endlessly.

When you begin observing and hunting humans, you will notice that they often face the same problems time and time again. If a human has an angry boss, he will quit his job and find another angry boss. If colleagues bully him, he will be bullied wherever he works. The same dysfunctional pattern of behaviour also occurs with humans who are often let down by friends or move from one 'batshit crazy' partner to another. Jealous humans, too, always seem to find something to be envious of. The same applies to paranoid humans or those who continually get into arguments and can't explain why.

<u>What makes humans so dysfunctional?</u>
From what we have presented until now, a human's filtered reality (his ability to notice certain things and his selective attention) is a culprit.

<u>First – Alternative Reality:</u> Every individual human being will tend to pay attention to things — objects and situations — that others may not be aware of or care about. Also, based on each human's background and experience, they can *notice* different things and details while in the same situation. So, as previously said, humans see reality differently. Remember, reality is complex, so there is always something happening around humans that allow them to reach the conclusions that they desire. No matter what the situation, humans can always find some reason to be anxious, paranoid or jealous, etc. The world really is unique for each of these creatures. Dare we say, humans see what they look for and understanding this fact will help you recognise the problems they face.
There are two other reasons for the problems humans grapple with. Let's look at them now.

<u>Secondly – Desire:</u> Each human has a pattern of desire, so he is attracted to and finds pleasure in the same things. Without noticing, humans usually chase the same type of humans over and over again. So, it's often their desire — what they chase — that creates the reoccurring problems humans complain about. It is like a human with a partner that ignores him. He always complains about being "invisible", but it's an inattentive partner he chased in the first place. In this case, should the partner begin paying him more attention, the human will lose interest and start looking for a new, less attentive mate. And, the problem continues.

<u>Thirdly – Behaviour:</u> Without noticing, humans also create problems

by the way they behave. For example, some highly competitive humans take an aggressive approach to others. Consequently, they appear confrontational, even when they don't mean to be. Why? Well, it's their belligerent body language, pronunciation of words and several other signals they can't help but project. Then, from time to time, they meet others who act the same, and, naturally, these aggressive humans end up in conflict. Many have no idea that they are part of the problem, that they created the fight, and so they blame their opponent.

Strangely, for the cases above, these patterns are habitual, and humans don't notice the cause. For human beings, life is a mystery. They are like creatures with shit on their foreheads that don't understand why flies follow them, no matter how many they swat away. Humans can't comprehend that, most often, they are the architect of their problems. And, like we said, the same happens with humans who are anxious, jealous or paranoid.

***

Tip: Pay attention to the problems a human continually faces; by doing so, you will uncover clues for preparing the tastiest bait. After all, given that humans have a tenuous grasp of reality, imagine all the gaps you can fill and buttons you can push with comments and innuendo.

***

Another practical application
LISTEN TO THE WORDS OF YOUR PREY

Note: Before we continue, it's important to highlight that, as a hunter, you mustn't jump to conclusions based on single events. Instead, wait and look for the consistency of any phenomena. For example, we will explore criticism. Now, one disparaging comment isn't enough to jump to a conclusion; frequent criticisms, however, are a more reliable indication of what's happening in a human's mind.

Now, let's explore some of the communication features we just explained. By knowing that the codes humans use to communicate are highly inefficient, it's easy to understand why words betray so much about them, and why you can use what they say against them.

You see, given the limited amount of information a human can process and express, you can learn plenty from what he says. A human's words expose the core of his reality and reveal a glimpse of what information he pays attention to and how he filters it.

If you are not convinced, follow the rationale in the following paragraphs. It's like a funnel. Imagine there are three levels of reality that get filtered (smaller and smaller) in the process.

The 3 levels of the funnel:
1. The *captured* reality that is detected by each human's sensors (eyes, ears, etc.).
2. The *perceived* reality (a small part of level 1) that the brain processes. This is the core — what he pays attention to.
3. The *commented* reality (a small part of level 2), which is the part humans choose to talk about — the core of the core.

As mentioned, humans grasp but a fraction of what's going on (captured reality) and then filter it their own way (perceived reality). Then, they use this small portion to make comments (commented reality). As you can imagine, what humans talk about should expose the crumb of reality they pay attention to. However, it gets better. Knowing what a human values is essential when deciding which trap and bait to use.

We say that humans can "choose" to talk about their reality. Why? Well, given human communication (words) is inefficient for expressing fully what a human observes and thinks, he must choose which portion of his reality to discuss. After all, it would be impossible to comment on and describe everything in detail. Understand this: Words are just a means for communicating to the world a slither of the information the Captain receives. Therefore, hunters should pay attention to what their prey says because, through their words, they are expressing the fraction of reality they see and how they see it.

You can use your human prey's words to understand what is important enough for him to notice and comment on. Listen to what he says because you will glean amazing clues for which bait to use to lure him — especially if his words are loaded with emotions like anger.

Think about a human who talks incessantly about money or

complains about others flaunting their wealth. This human is usually unaware that he is revealing that money seems extremely important to him, and the trap you prepare should take this into account.

You see, the human has noticed the wealth of another and, among all the things happening around him, has chosen this particular thing to complain about. You can use this rationale for pretty much anything a human criticises: homosexuals, humans who are too tall or thin, humans who have had plastic surgery or don't wear certain clothes. What do these criticisms tell you about the humans who speak of them?

As a rule, the things one human criticises another about reveal clues for what you can use against him. When a human criticises something, he is also, in an indirect way, saying he is not that. Or, in other words, he is better than that. Beware, though: Indirectly, he is saying the topic is important to him. He can also be revealing what he is interested in and what he is afraid of being perceived as — *"I hate homosexuals."* Really? Sure you do, buddy!

But don't be mistaken. We are not saying a human who criticises a homosexual necessarily wants to be one. You can't immediately define your bait based on just that. Instead, we are highlighting that homosexuality seems important to him, to the point that he feels he should comment about it while others would rather speak about other things. Of course, his commenting on the topic can make you wonder why he finds it so important. The same applies to humans who hate immigrants or humans of a different race. Why is their attention directed to these things? As a hunter, this is the question to ask.

When observing your prey constantly criticising something, take notes. Only by gathering data can you determine the right bait to use; you must understand what resonates with your human quarry. You need lots of data because criticisms can lead you to false conclusions. For example, a human can complain about his boss, but he is actually sad about his career. Or, another human might complain about his partner, but, in fact, he is disappointed with himself. So, you mustn't take a human's words at face value. For now, think of complaints as clues to go with others to form a complete picture.

***

<u>Tip:</u> Remember that human beings are aware of only a fragment of what

happens around them. So, whatever a human talks about reveals what he pays attention to. Listen to what he says, and especially to what he complains about, and you will discover the best bait for your hunt.

***

TAKEAWAYS

The Captain is ISOLATED inside the Cabin, receiving poor and tainted information about the outside world, and he is unable to express himself fully. After all, what a human says is a poor facsimile of everything happening in his mind. So, the things humans frequently criticise reveal a lot about them. Pay attention and keep notes.

Most problems humans experience are recurrent because of what they desire, how they behave and how their minds filter reality. So, keep an eye on the pattern of their reoccurring problems. Doing so can provide great insights.

So, whenever you interact with humans, bear in mind that they can't fully express themselves or grasp reality. And, when being hunted, ignorance of this truth can be fatal.

Anyway, enough with the basics. Now, armed with a new mindset about humans, you are ready to learn even more about this fascinating prey. In the next part, we will now dig deeper into humans' alternative realities.

PART II
DIGGING DEEPER INTO YOUR PREY'S REALITY

6

HAUNTED BY MEANINGS
HIDDEN ASSOCIATIONS

So, human communication is a mess, and Earth's smartest animals live in different realities. One consequence (among many) is that each human continues to face the same problems over and over again.

We will now explore another feature that affects how humans perceive reality in a major way. As you will see in this chapter, the meanings humans attach to things and situations vary widely among them and profoundly affect how they perceive their surroundings. To complicate things further, humans are unaware of the associations they make. We know it sounds strange, but they really are oblivious. As you will see, associations are hidden, and so humans don't realise they 'see' different things. We will show you why and how this happens.

As a result of this phenomenon, two humans exposed to the same situation can interpret it in ways that are so unalike that you will be incredulous, even when we explain why.

A warning before we begin:
We know you must be anxious to start playing with humans' fear, which is fun, indeed. However, to really understand the source of humans' conflicts and struggles, we must delve into the reasons why they perceive

35

different realities.

So, this chapter and the next are more complicated than those so far. Why? Well, let's just say that a human's thoughts and actions can be compensatory substitutes for desires he doesn't even know he has, which, consequently, make them difficult to spot.

For this chapter and the next, therefore, *resilience* is the word. If it helps, we assure you that this chapter's topic, Hidden Associations, should be easier to understand once read along with the following chapter, *The Drawers*. Both are related. In this chapter, we explore the twisted meanings things and situations have for humans, which, when understood along with the categories (Drawers) of the human mind are powerful for understanding human behaviour.

As usual, we will start with an exaggerated example to illustrate the idea:

<u>Tell a human this story: Multiple and personal codebooks</u>
Imagine two ships displaying flags. Lookouts on each vessel observe the flags and report what they see to their respective messengers who each have a list of flag codes and their meanings.

Or, imagine two castles communicating using smoke signals. In both situations, the lookouts and messengers interpret the signals and explain the meaning to their captains.

As already discussed, communication problems are inevitable. Overall, though, the messages would be understood, right?

What would happen, though, if each ship or castle had different codebooks and were not aware of the fact? "My God!" you say. "It would be a mess!" Yes, any human can see the problems this system would create — especially if the captains were oblivious to the codes' different meanings.

<u>How does this apply to humans? And how can you use it against them?</u>
Do you know that every human has an inbuilt codebook to decipher his environment? It's true. And, like the messengers' interpretations, each human's book of codes is different. Consequently, humans appear to be talking about the same thing, but many times they are not. So, it is possible to observe completely different behaviours between humans facing the same situations.

It is important to point out again that, most of the time, the Captain is oblivious to the fact that the information he receives is misleading or entirely false. And, as discussed in previous chapters, when the Messenger manipulates information *en route* to the Captain, anything can become reality.

To understand, first we should demonstrate some simple examples of how the same situation (or flag or smoke signal) can have alternative meanings to different groups of humans.

DIFFERENT ASSOCIATIONS AT GROUP LEVEL

Let's look at a few everyday situations:

In some parts of Earth, getting a tan is considered desirable and leads to more social approval. There, white humans sunbathe or apply artificial methods to darken their skin.

Meanwhile, in other places, chalk-white skin is considered more attractive; some humans actually inject substances into their veins to achieve this goal.

So, a human from one part of the planet (like China) will have an opposing idea of desirable skin colour than one from another part (like Brazil). Both humans share the same goal, but to look good or be sexy, one hides from the sun while the other chases it.

Therefore, the same pallid skin can transform from not at all attractive to 'drop-dead gorgeous' when the information reaches the Captain. Yes, skin colour can have opposite meanings for different groups of humans.

In another example, a human dines at another's house. He eats everything served, leaving not a solitary crumb on his plate. Depending on the culture, his actions could be considered either polite or rude.

You see, in some parts of Earth, eating everything served is considered polite; it means the food was good. Those of other cultures, though, would think the human is implying that his host didn't serve enough. Yes! The meaning and potential for disappointments and misunderstandings of a few missing crumbs at dinner can vary depending on the group of humans you are dealing with and which codes they use to interpret the world.

In a last example, paying a restaurant bill can be viewed as a show of respect and appreciation, or an attempt to dominate. It gets interesting when a human tries to demonstrate one thing, and the other understands the complete opposite. Often, the offended human can't understand or believe that his interpretation isn't what the 'offender' meant.

Misunderstandings happen between cultures, despite humans knowing that interpretations of things and situations can vary widely. Imagine how intriguing it can get when humans don't realise that different meanings occur between close friends and family? Yes, what they usually don't grasp is that definitions also vary within the same community — even the same family. And, most of the time, those who do understand this truth don't appreciate the depth of the issue.

The same applies to several other behaviours, and the broader the meaning of a word, activity, gesture or situation, the wider the difference can get.

For humans, money, a career, success, power, sex, marriage, fidelity, intimacy, betrayal, family, friendships, freedom, change, uncertainty, the forbidden, rejections, failures, death, religion and politics all have wildly different meanings — even between family members.

When hunting, aim to know, better than your prey, what things such as power or marriage represent to him. Always ask, *"What does this mean to my human quarry, and what does he associate with it?"*

Let's now explain how you can identify your prey's associations.

HIDDEN ASSOCIATIONS

Check out the following examples. Keep in mind that they represent just some possible meanings (that each human can associate with a situation), and, depending on the human's interpretation, there are many others.

<u>A discussion can be an exchange of ideas or a chance to see who is best</u>: If a human associates a discussion with a chance to see who is the best, like a battle, it's not surprising he will be defensive and refuse to change his mind, even when presented with undeniable facts. In this case, he will listen to arguments, not to reflect, but to identify flaws to attack, and he will be immune to reason. This human is a 'gladiator', and finding a solution or the truth isn't his 'thing'. At the same time, if the human associates discussion with an exchange of ideas to discover the truth, he will act differently in the same situation.

Once you recognise, what we call "Hidden Associations", it's easy to understand some behaviours. Let's look at some other examples:

<u>A human gives advice that isn't followed</u>: In this situation, a particular kind of creature will get extremely 'pissed' because refusal to heed his advice is a 'clear sign' of disrespect. He doesn't know, but for him, not having his advice followed suggests he has no control over other humans or that they don't care for his guidance. For others, though, having their advice followed, or not, has no association with disrespect or a lack of control. It's just advice. Consequently, not being adhered to is no big deal. *"Hey, at the end of the day, they can do what they want!"*

<u>Money can be a currency to trade, a measure of success or compensation for a weakness</u>: So, as expected, when faced with the possibility of losing money, humans can react in many different ways — even two equally wealthy humans. All due to the meanings each human associates with losing money. For one, who uses money to compensate for some insecurity, even losing a few dollars can be devastating.

Looking at the three examples above, a clueless human would think that the topic of discussion, the advice provided, or the amount of financial loss, is the problem. However, for humans, life is far more complicated than that. In reality, what matters in the first example could be who wins; in the second, who is in control may be what counts; and, in the third example, the weaknesses or insecurities that a financial 'hit' exposes, and what winning or losing means, could be the cause of anxiety.

And the list goes on and on.

A luxury item, like jewellery or a car, can represent a symbol of success and social status to some humans. Alternatively, depending on how the owner displays his 'bling', for others he can be seen as a needy individual begging for social approval and recognition.

Also, a human might speak of his desire to own a business, but, in fact, he longs for freedom and recognition, not to be an entrepreneur. Read between the lines to understand what humans are *really* talking about.

Two humans spend months — even years — grieving the death of their offspring. Eventually, the father starts 'living' again; however, the mother continues to mourn. This situation causes tension between the couple. For the father, the death is a tragedy that will linger for the rest of his life, but, regardless, he wants to be happy again. For the mother, however, a return to happiness could mean she doesn't love her offspring enough, and, in this case, if she starts enjoying life again, it wasn't valuable enough to be remembered — she'd be a terrible mother. Can you see how far things can get? In this case, the mother views her partner's perspective as disrespectful, a threat to the worthiness of their child's life. She, however, isn't fully aware of where her anger originates.

DIFFERENT MEANINGS IN HUMAN RELATIONSHIPS

A human can be considered attractive because he is fashionable (dresses well) and has a muscular body. Alternatively, an unfashionable slob can be viewed as a 'good catch' because he appears traditional, less influenced by fads and more likely to be stable in a relationship. And, just like the other cases, of course, humans are usually unaware of all the associations behind whom they find attractive — they just know they find another either 'hot' or not.

In the same way, a human can choose a partner because he (or she) is charismatic and strong. Or, he can love her because of a weakness — some disability or illness. How come? Well, to this human, a 'flawed' mate could make him feel more important and safe; in his mind, she is less likely to abandon him for another. So, he sees a weakness and is attracted to the possibility of feeling important and powerful (being needed and able to help). He might also relish the opportunity of being in a stable relationship. But, the human won't recognise his motivations; he just knows that he likes the other human who just happens to have a weakness.

Generally speaking, you might presume that a human will be attracted to another who treats him with respect and allows freedom in a relationship. Some poor souls, though, are turned on by dominant, disrespectful partners whom they see as superior to themselves. In these cases, a show of respect could be perceived as a sign of weakness — a real turn off. Yes, it can get as crazy as that. And, in both cases, fixing the 'problem' (curing the weak partner or convincing the dominant one to show respect) could threaten the relationship.

Here's one more example that is a bit less obvious: A heterosexual female human could be attracted to homosexual males because they don't desire her. Simple as that. We will show you two possible reasons:

First, deep down, she may believe that if she succeeds in her seduction, she will feel more wanted and beautiful, which is intensely arousing to her. After all, this guy doesn't even like women! If she can 'get into the sack' a man who isn't attracted to the opposite sex, what does that mean about her? She must be mind-blowingly amazing, that's what! Of course, she won't admit, or even be aware of, her reason for pursuing homosexual men and may make all kinds of assumptions about the reasons behind her desire.

Or, here's another possible reason for the attraction: At Crew level, the female may imagine that she will be able to be more aggressive during sex and assume that her homosexual partner won't respond with force. In this case, she might find the fantasy of full expression, without the typical consequences of aggressive behaviour, enticing. Here again, the human will most probably be unaware of all her assumptions, unless she investigates her thoughts at a deeper level — which almost never happens.

So, of course, we have used extreme examples to show the power of Hidden Associations. As you can see, they can drive humans to make significant life decisions without knowing the assumptions that lead to them.

Now, return to the last few paragraphs where we explained a female human's attraction to homosexual males and re-read them a couple of times. Can you see any problems? Probably not. However, believe us, the fact that we used a female, instead of, as usual, a male to explain our point can, for some humans, mean we are misogynistic. They won't just imply this understanding, either; they will be absolutely certain. The thing to understand is that Hidden Associations can be radically different from human to human, but the outcome is usually powerful. Humans reach important conclusions with a minimal understanding of the reasons why. They don't treat it as a possibility, but most often as a logical and certain conclusion.

In another example, a human's partner could be a best friend with sex, a housekeeper, a substitute for his mother, a trophy or the reason for living — a saviour and guardian of happiness. With these alternative associations, how different do you think human behaviour can be?

Let's say that marriage can mean a contract that establishes the rules of a partnership or, alternatively, a symbol of ultimate success — the source of happiness. It is easy to see why humans react differently to the same relationship problems. For one partner, the threat of breaking up is far more distressing than for the other; therefore, each will react differently to a troubled relationship.

There are countless examples, and all because humans think everybody reads from the same codebook; they are confident that their, often erroneous, conclusions are correct. Just like a human who reads the wrong map and feels sure he is heading in the right direction, a wrong book of codes misleads a human's interpretation of the world. So, often, humans' Captains are receiving the wrong information and perceiving alternative realities.

Here is a funny situation: A female human asks her partner to wash the dishes and a refusal, or him doing a poor job, could cause trouble. Why? Possibly because, to her, the chore represents many other meanings, like how much he still cares about their relationship and whether there is still love. So, by refusing to wash the dishes or doing a poor job, her partner is secretly and unconsciously sending a far worse message than he thinks.

The same happens if a human complains about his partner's cooking. Fair enough, no? Actually, she is livid for apparently no reason. And, eventually, the couple discuss whether they still love each other, whether they should remain together — all because of a meal! It is possible that the human's partner concludes that not liking the food is a clue to a much broader meaning, which, again, both humans are unaware of. We kid you not.

CONTINUALLY CHANGING UNCHANGEABLE TRUTHS

Interestingly, most humans are unaware that what they believe to be universal truths have changed over time.

For example, among humans, dominance during sex is currently associated with being on top; in days gone by, however, dominating meant being beneath a partner. So, two humans who both want to be in the 'driver's seat' can do so in opposite ways: one can be on top, and the other can achieve the same goal on the bottom.

In another example, currently, the size of a male human's genitalia is usually related to power; it is commonly desired to be longer and bigger. In contrast, a large appendage was once considered something to be ashamed of — a characteristic of slaves.

Desired body shapes have also changed throughout history. So, many of the 'truths' humans believe are simply a product of their generation, and yet they act as if they have always been so. As a result, it becomes even more difficult for them to question the assumptions in their minds.

But, why don't humans recognise that they interpret the same stuff differently?

Let's investigate why and where this phenomenon starts.

***

Tip: If your prey reacts unexpectedly, he probably isn't crazy; instead, he likely has an alternative interpretation of a situation. Rule of thumb, and remembering the previous chapters, if a human overreacts to something, he is probably linking it to other meanings.

***

AN ANCIENT & ESSENTIAL FEATURE

It is important to note that Hidden Associations (or simply inner Shortcuts) are not all bad. In fact, many are necessary because they allow humans to react quickly to things and situations without expending much cerebral energy. For example, in the jungle, if a human sees a lion, he will most likely (if he's smart) associate it with danger — the human will feel fear, his heart will pound, and he will run. Similarly, when a human sees an animal with red skin, he may conclude it is poisonous.

Though often necessary, the problem with Shortcuts is that humans are addicted to the fast, easy way of seeing the world, and they can't kick the habit.

You see, a human who spots a red-skinned animal may not know for sure that it is poisonous. However, he chooses not to touch it because determining whether it is 100% safe takes more energy than making an assumption. The red skin and the lion are facts; whether or not the two creatures are dangerous are assumptions that can be true or false. And, humans struggle to differentiate automatic assumptions from facts — during caveman days, stopping to decide whether or not a creature is a predator could be fatal, something of a health hazard.

The human brain assigns meanings to the stuff. Not just often, but always. So, that is not just a lion; it is a predator and danger all at once.

It's true that analysing a situation objectively is difficult and energy-intensive for humans. In modern times, though, analysis at least avoids wrong conclusions such as:

- *"He refused to wash the dishes today, so he doesn't love me."*
- *"The human is poor, so he's a loser."*
- *"He's rich, so he's a winner."*
- *"He's gay, so he's a freak."*

You can imagine, however, that analysis does bring complexity and uncertainty into humans' lives. And, these smart primates need assumptions because of their limited view of the world.

Assumptions can be small, like a human walking and assuming the floor will still be there when he takes his next step. Or, they can be more complicated: *"That guy is frowning at me; he must want a fight."*

Like the innate fear of lions and red-skinned animals, some assumptions are essential for survival. For example, a human sees an angry dog and immediately assumes he should find a place to hide. Or, if a human sees another approaching wearing strange clothing and holding an axe, he presumes that this odd character is trouble, so he crosses the street.

Humans make assumptions based on their experiences, which, when fleeing from a lion or an axe-wielding weirdo, is a sound life-preserving strategy. However, very few humans are cognisant of the assumptions they make, and only awareness will enable them to ask questions such as, *"Is wealth really an indication of intelligence?"* or *"Is washing the dishes a proxy for love?"* Humans make so many incorrect assumptions that they are not even aware of.

Assumptions often lead some humans to conclude that kindness is weakness and brutality is power; a want is a need and something that is common is normal, which then becomes the right thing to do. Some humans even directly link uncertainty with danger. Most can't see that all these associations can be both right and wrong. For example, kindness can indicate weakness, but, at the same time, a kind-hearted human can just as likely be 'hard as nails'. By not jumping to conclusions you can uncover the truth.

One of the most intriguing and misleading conclusions humans come to is that 'ranting and raving', and trying to impose one's will on others, is a sign of power. Most often, though, in a group of humans, the one who makes the most noise is the weakest and the one who feels most vulnerable. It's true: Humans who feel compelled to demonstrate their power at higher decibels usually doubt whether they have any power at all.

As you can see, a small sign can be viewed as related to strength or weakness, depending on Hidden Associations.

In one last example, a common situation, especially in humans nearing maturity, is doing 'forbidden' things often connected to feeling more free and mature. So, not surprisingly, young humans do one thing when they actually seek something seemingly unrelated. For example, sometimes, an obedient human (good student) can fall in love with the 'wrong' type (troubled student). Dating the troubled student (against the rules) makes the good student feel more mature. Got it? Of course, the good student isn't aware of what's going on, but most often what the animal is really in love with is the feeling of adulthood, not the other human. In this case, to forbid the good student from meeting the other (an object of love) will just 'stoke the fire' — increase the animal's ardour. After all, the more repressed a human animal is, the more it will desire to be free, given the link it makes. Crazy, wouldn't you say?

So, as a hunter, you should always keep this in mind — that all things that lead to assumptions should not be treated as conclusions. Not as certainties, but as probabilities. The world is complicated, with infinite possibilities.

WHERE DO THESE CRAZY ASSOCIATIONS COME FROM?

In this book so far, we have often explained the reasons for problems to help you understand the opportunities they offer. So, we will here, too. However, we won't spend much time on this; if we do, we run the risk of our book looking like a self-help guide for losers. Nevertheless, you can't underestimate the power of Hidden Associations if exploited well, so it is of paramount importance that you have a solid understanding of them.

After all, when it comes to a human's mind, most of its 'shape' was usually sculpted in his early years. His past flows within him and at a deeper level than you might think.

Let's start with an unusual metaphor:

<u>Tell a human this story: Born on an alien planet</u>

Imagine you were born on another planet. You are confused, and the animal you are has two heads, eight paws, some weird extra sensors and other peculiar appendages that you need to get used to. Not only is your body alien to you, so is the planet that you call home. The gravity is different, and it's hard to breathe — maybe you are underwater? You can see other creatures like you, and they communicate using strange sounds and gestures that you can't comprehend.

In this situation, how lost would you be? And, how many wrong conclusions would you make based on observing the strange creatures and world around you?

Oh, wait. Maybe this example is too 'far out' for the human imagination. Perhaps it is better to describe another example that humans can cope with.

Imagine a human who has never left his country. He accepts an invitation to a ritual called a "wedding", or some traditional festival in another country, one of which he knows nothing about its culture (for example, an American attending a wedding in China or India, or vice versa).

The human has zero knowledge of the foreign country's language, so during the ritual, he pays particular attention to the local behaviours. He observes the way the humans dress and how they greet each other. He notices that these strange creatures drink hot water and tea, instead of the cold water or beer with which he's familiar. They sit differently, too — leaning forward like they are about to erupt into an argument — and this posture gives him a weird impression. Slowly, the human begins to paint a mental picture of how things work in this strange land — how to behave to be accepted, how to win a partner, what he shouldn't do.

Needless to say, the human will most likely reach many wrong conclusions due to misinterpreting situations. Because he doesn't understand the culture and language, he will continue making incorrect assumptions that might lead to trouble for him later.

How does this apply to humans? And how can you use it against them?

So, as you know, humans are from Earth. But, at the time of their birth, their planet is like an alien world to them. Everything is new. They must learn how to breathe, eat — even come to grips with gravity. Humans underestimate how they once were, and confusion lingers for many years.

Most Hidden Associations develop when young. You see, human infants have enormous imaginations, mainly because they don't yet understand Earth's rules. In a young human's mind, one little thing can draw many weird images and conclusions. He hasn't even mastered his inefficient communication system yet. Imagine the extent to which a lack of understanding, blended with a full dependency on others, can shape a young human's assumptions about the world. This is how Shortcuts begin, and human infants grow into maturity blind to their existence.

Some experiences and memories are suppressed during a human's early years, not intentionally, but because they are too hard to cope with. Consequently, humans become masters of deception in order to avoid unpleasant experiences, and they use the techniques of denial and blame. They ignore problems (like the ones presented in the Weak Captain example) or keep busy to avoid thinking about them.

However, the memories remain. And, during a human's lifetime, whenever a situation arises that resembles a bad memory, an internal explosion occurs, which seems to come from nothing. He doesn't really know what's wrong; he just loses his temper.

Suppressed memories offer enormous opportunities for hunters, although it can be difficult to understand the full picture. Just to be clear, we are not talking about significant trauma-causing childhood events (they are too obvious). You wouldn't believe how random these associations can be. Siblings, for example, can have different perspectives on life. During a human's early years, small misunderstandings can snowball.

While in childhood, humans create assumptions that lead to Shortcuts relating to social patterns for things like security, social acceptance, how to treat others and what is success and failure — the basis of what shapes their behaviours and desires throughout life. These early assumptions are the seeds of the Hidden Associations mentioned in the previous examples.

Finally, it is also important to remember that all human parents were once children, so they also have a legacy of strange associations from their early years influencing them. As a result, throughout human history, there is a chain of events with cause and effect passed from generation to generation. You won't need much time to observe how humans train their young (called education) in their first years to see how bad it can get. After all, humans are ill-equipped to manage their lives. But, if you do want to check it out, you will see parents compensating for their sorrows by pressuring their offspring, creating unreasonable expectations, lying for no reason and creating unnecessary disappointments. You will also see absent, insecure or needy parents playing a significant role in their kids' education — all to your advantage. So, having these kinds of 'teachers' during their early years, how flawed do you think the associations that humans have can get? We think you know the answer.

In summary, Hidden Associations are a big flaw to exploit. Just pay attention to each human's reactions to situations. Let's check out a simple consequence of an association that can haunt humans for life using an example similar to one already described. Now, though, we will focus on the possible source of the problem.

Let's return to the human with a disrespectful partner. You may ask why would he be attracted to a mate who ignores him and treats him like garbage? Yes, for some human animals, a disrespectful partner feels familiar — perhaps evokes memories of their parents. Or, maybe the human believes he'd never win a valuable partner who also shows kindness, so a partner who is 'easy to get' seems less desirable.

Yes, it goes that far. And, this human will be blind to why he finds such a partner attractive. If you recall the Repetition feature already explained, it is easy to expect the human to jump from one toxic relationship to another. Rather than bad luck, the reason he ends up with obnoxious partners is his 'toxic' attraction created in his early years by his parents and education.

Let's look at the source of the problem in another example.

<u>Different reactions towards small mistakes:</u> It can make a massive difference to a human's life if, in his early years, he believes his caregivers accept (love) him unconditionally. You see, knowing he will be loved regardless of success or failure gives him emotional security. On the other hand, a human who believes his caregivers' love is conditional, based on him meeting certain expectations, will live in constant alert mode. Naturally for him, and most often, even a small mistake can mean big trouble, and his insecurity will usually lead to all kinds of strange behaviours, like blaming others and denial. So, for this 'conditionally loved' human, there is much at stake with every action he takes, and he gets nervous whenever he makes a mistake. Even an innocuous critique can cause a flood of emotions due to all the meanings it represents.

So, this is where crazy associations that lead to unfathomable conclusions come from. Pay attention to a human's behaviour in a particular situation — you'll get some useful clues.

***

<u>Tip:</u> Whenever you see your prey complaining about something, try to see how similar the situation is to a problem from his past. For example, he complains that his boss does something (it could be anything, something small, like lack of attention or recognition) that irritates him profoundly. Then, investigate whether one of his parents used to do the same thing. Many times you will find striking similarities between both events. Why does this happen? Well, in a case like this, what irritates the human most is not the problem but the fact that he is facing it again — even though, as usual, he is unaware of the connection.

***

Perhaps the human is super sensitive because the problem he experiences with his boss reminds him how his father used to treat him.

49

It's like the issue never goes away — remember the Repetition feature?

And, of course, another human who never faced the problem when young probably won't be bothered by the boss's actions or behaviour.

In the same way, humans who are violent as adults usually faced big challenges in their formative years. As one can expect, based on what we explained, usually before becoming 'monsters', they were wounded children haunted by, and fighting, problems of the past. Their associations are all messed up.

THE HUMAN BRAIN'S ASSOCIATIONS CAN HAVE OPPOSITE & UNEXPECTED MEANINGS

To complicate matters further, it is possible for your prey to have not just slightly different, but totally opposite, meanings related to the same thing. As usual, it all comes down to what something means to each human.

For example, feeling pain (which one would naturally expect should be avoided) can lead a human to believe he is winning. And, so, he can enjoy it. The way a human views pain can considerably change his perception of, and interaction with, reality. You see, all kinds of links can happen. Suffering can mean something to be avoided, or it can have a good connotation.

Consider the following examples:
- Pain after exercising can feel good if the human links it to improving his body.
- Or, sacrifice (for religious purposes or some other cause) can be a sign of achievement, leading the human to believe he is different (better) than others who don't forgo life's comforts. Therefore, the human abstains from eating something he loves (meat or dairy, for example), and he feels good.

So, humans can suffer and feel better — they can take pleasure from sacrifice. In a simple example, the sacrifices of religion can be pleasurable if a human links them to getting closer to his god or paradise (a concept of afterlife for some humans).

Consequently, a religion can dictate that followers make sacrifices and follow certain rules. These followers will feel good because the rules and sacrifices have alternative and deeper meanings than just the pain you see on the surface. Also, obeying makes them feel like part of a group with a common cause that brings them a step closer to heaven, etc. Can you see all the rewards attached to sacrifice due to the meaning some humans can link to it?

So, these humans suffer and feel good, which sounds contradictory. As you can see, humans will react to situations depending on how each interprets things around them. Always dig deeper and ask yourself, *"What does something mean for my prey?"*

IT TAKES A LONG TIME TO DEMOLISH A HUMAN'S DEEP-SEATED SHORTCUTS

In the case of a human who links discussion to battle, it's not too hard to change his association. And, by doing so, it is possible to alter his attitude and behaviour towards having a discussion. However, remember that most associations are made by the Crew at a deep level, not the Captain. So, for humans, a Shortcut is challenging to identify and fix because, even if their Captain knows about it, he still must slowly explain it to his Messenger who is strongly influenced by past experiences. Otherwise, the Messenger will continue to send the Captain the wrong message.

Here's an example of an association that is difficult to destroy. Remember when we explained the Repetition feature, the human who is attracted to partners who ignore him? Well, even if he understood the reasons for his attraction, he would still need the strength of Hercules (one of Earth's mythical warriors) to change. Yes, it would take a huge amount of effort to adjust, and the human will possibly never completely alter what turns him on. However, he can compromise. You see, once the human becomes aware of his unhealthy association, he could seek a human who, like previous partners, appears to ignore him (he likes that) because she is introverted, quiet and shy. However, unlike previous partners, she does care for him.

Given how difficult it is for humans to change their meanings, don't worry if some stumble upon this book; they will have difficulty questioning or changing the meanings inside their heads. It would take a long time and lots of effort for what we say to sink in. As explained, humans live with Hidden Associations (and categories, as we will explain in the next chapter) for so long that they become part of their identity.

So, for humans, questioning their meanings is like challenging their identity and would lead to feelings of uncertainty, which the human brain hates. Humans will fight 'tooth and nail' against uncertainty — they'll even ignore evidence that is contrary to their beliefs and cling to small truths that indicate they are right. In almost all cases, humans are emotionally invested in preserving their ignorance of inner, unsettling truths.

The similarities between these examples, and the Weak Captain using blame and denial, are not a coincidence. Remember that the world is complicated, so humans can find evidence for almost anything, from religious beliefs to jealousy and how they choose their partners. Like we mentioned before, humans become immune to reason.

TO CONCLUDE BEFORE WE JUMP INTO THE DRAWERS

So, humans' multiple codebooks lead to many possible interpretations of the same situations. Earth's most advanced primates are oblivious to this truth and often can't separate assumptions from facts.

It's like they view the world through sunglasses, unaware that every single pair has different coloured lenses. One human wears blue, the other pink. So, one will see blue stuff, and everything to the other will be rose-tinted. Like most humans, these two wouldn't be aware they see different colours. It's true that some humans are aware of the situation, but even they usually have a hard time applying this knowledge to their lives.

As if that isn't enough, it gets more complicated or irrational (but also useful from a hunter's perspective) because there is an additional human feature that alters their reality even more, one that can potentially multiply the problem several times. We're talking about the way humans process and organise information. In the next chapter, we explain why some small changes in meanings can catapult widely different and extreme conclusions that lead humans to develop kinds of Allergies to certain words and situations.

Lastly, remember that when you observe your prey doing anything (especially if it's odd and unexpected), always ask, *"What does it mean to this animal?"*

7

THE EXTREMES
HUMAN DRAWERS

As if the Hidden Associations aren't crazy enough, here's another reality-distorting human feature: These creatures organise information within their heads into categories — like drawers.

So, after assigning meaning to a situation, humans categorise it. Given that they usually have very few categories (often just two to analyse a specific situation, as we will explain), one small thing can transform a situation from being perceived as excellent to awful.

In this chapter, we use Drawers as a metaphor for categories. Doing so will enable us to demonstrate how an even slightly different meaning between humans can lead to massive differences in how each perceives reality. These Drawers multiply the problems that start with the Hidden Associations. Also, using the Drawers metaphor will help you understand why human perception can, in the blink of an eye, shift from good to bad, all to nothing, and — winner to loser.

Yes, humans can instantly change how they label situations and how they behave towards them. Wait and see.

CLARIFICATION

The human mind is so odd that we must remind you that what we are about to explain is not based solely on our decades of experience in dealing with humans. You can also find the knowledge we share in their books. What we explain is a practical and simple interpretation, especially for hunters while on Earth, of a highly complex concept.

THE EXTREMES

Let's start with an exaggerated example that summarises features related to both this chapter and the last:

<u>Tell a human this story: The prisoner</u>
Imagine a human in a squalid, overcrowded prison. There is no middle ground in this hell hole; either the human is a murderer, a rapist or a victim of those kinds of criminals. As you can expect, being categorised as a victim would be a nightmare. So, once confined to this prison, even innocent humans (those wrongly sentenced) see no alternative but to do whatever it takes to avoid being labelled as a victim — they become real criminals.
Do you get the picture so far?
Now, imagine that in this prison, any hint of weak or loser behaviour can lead to a prisoner being categorised as a victim by other inmates, which is almost equivalent to a death sentence. Yes, within seconds, a murderer to be feared can be reclassified as a victim to be preyed upon. So, it is natural to imagine that those criminals perceived as tough live in constant alert mode and feel unable to show any flaws. They must always be the criminal; any sign of weaknesses can be fatal.

<u>How does this apply to humans? And how can you use it against them?</u>
Any human would shudder at this nightmare situation. It's not only the thought of incarceration that is chilling but the idea of being haunted day and night by fears of being perceived as a victim.

If you told a human that in their daily lives the vast majority of his kind live a similar nightmare, he wouldn't understand.

How come?

Let's start from the beginning.

Humans continuously categorise everything they see or pay attention to. You see, labelling things and situations helps them understand quickly what's happening around them. But, for hunters, what's most fascinating is that humans usually have too few categories, or Drawers, as we describe them, and so they must adapt. Yes, for many humans, their brain has minimal Drawers, so they label things based on what they have. What other choice is there? As expected, this feature causes extreme behaviour because things get stuck in the duality of 0 or 100: good or bad, black or white; there is no middle ground.

For example, if a human had just two Drawers (black and white) he would have no choice but to place any colour he sees in one of the two. So, anything that isn't entirely white may be interpreted as black.

How does this all work in practical terms? Well, as mentioned, most humans have too few Drawers, so they label everything as either "winner" or "loser". With only two large Drawers in their minds, these humans live in perpetual fear of being perceived by themselves, or others, as a loser.

HOW DOES LABELLING HAPPEN?

Let's look at another exaggerated example that explains how labelling (putting things and situations into Drawers) works inside a human's mind — without him even knowing.

Labelling happens before humans receive information, so the message is compromised by the time it reaches the Captain.

We warn you that the following example, which explains the process of putting information into Drawers, is rather long and complicated. However, it needs to be to ensure you understand fully that categorising happens without a human knowing.

Tell a human this story: The Drawers

Imagine that the messenger, on the previously described ancient ship, relays information to the captain in his cabin. However, this time, for greater security, he writes the information on paper and sends it to the captain through a line-of-transaction drawer, also known as a pass-through.

We know this sounds crazy, but you'll get what we mean.

Now, on this ship, there are only two transaction drawers for the messenger to choose: one for good news (safe, winner, friends, etc.) and one for bad news (danger, loser, enemy, war, doomsday, etc.). Every time the messenger uses the bad-news drawer to inform the captain, a warning alarm for battle mode starts to ring — the ship is in danger and, therefore, vulnerable.

Note that the alarm rings BEFORE the captain reads the message.

As expected, the drawer in which the message is placed determines whether conditions are good or bad, whether the crew thinks the ship is in a winning or losing situation.

Now, let's say that the messenger, based on all his mind's past experiences and crazy associations, must decide whether news of an approaching ship should go into the good-news (safety) or bad-news (danger) drawer.

Interestingly, sometimes a small detail can determine which drawer the messenger sends the message through. If the messenger judges the approaching ship as a possible threat and chooses the bad-news drawer, even before the captain receives the message, the war-mode alarm will reverberate throughout the ship. The crew will become agitated and run to their positions. Sails and oars will be adjusted for battle and artillery (cannons and ammunition, etc.) prepared. All this will happen before the captain can even read the message. And, there is no middle ground; the ship will be full throttle into war mode.

<u>How does this apply to humans? And how can you use it against them?</u>
This example sounds complicated. But it shows that all decisions for which Drawer to place information into (how to label and store it in a human's memory) are made before the Captain receives it. The message is biased, tainted. Before a human truly understands a situation, his heart pounds, or he becomes angry, and all these reactions are mostly beyond his control at the time. Should the human have developed more Drawers, he would have better control.

The example also shows that the Drawers are not easy to change.

There is a structural problem to overcome. The captain would have to work with the messenger for months — even years — to construct new categories to receive better information.

In the same way, for example, it would be difficult for a human to create new Drawers overnight just by reading this book. It takes lots of time and effort to perceive reality through new Drawers.

WHEN HAVING FEW DRAWERS AFFECTS HUMANS' PERCEIVED REALITY

In a bar, a waiter ignores a male human for a couple of minutes. Though unaware, deep inside the male thinks, *"Do winners get ignored? No, they don't. So, this waiter is implying that I am a loser!"* Be aware, that for this human, "loser" is the only option for this situation. So, suddenly, a lack of attention becomes a challenge to his manhood, and the male creates an ugly scene. Yes, a few bad minutes have ruined a good night out. So, the male human (at the Messenger level) concludes that the waiter is calling him a loser and placing him in the Loser Drawer. And, he doesn't even realise the real reason behind his angst. He simply blames and hates the waiter.

In the same way, a minor traffic incident can be seen as a threat to a human's manhood and result in road rage — the guy who cut him off is labelling him a loser!

In a class presentation, students can present very different behaviours based on their interpretation of the occasion. Remember, as explained in the last chapter, whether a human feels he is loved conditionally or unconditionally can affect how he perceives a small mistake. So, a *faux pas* can have different meanings, which are also multiplied based on the number of Drawers a human has. You see, a class presentation can be an opportunity for a student to show his knowledge or, alternatively, a task to prove that he will be successful in life and justify his family's love and acceptance.

You see, to a human with just two Drawers, success means he is a winner, and a small flaw makes him a loser, afraid, unlovable and a social pariah. One Drawer holds many meanings. Suddenly, a class presentation becomes far more because there is so much to lose should the human happen to jump from one Drawer to the other.

All conclusions humans come to can be based on tiny clues. It is easy to understand why some step on stage for a presentation with their heart pounding like a gladiator prepared to kill or be killed at the Coliseum; there is so much at stake.

Drawers causing career troubles:
A boss might request something that the employee sees as too basic and dumb but still involves twenty minutes of extra work. So, following the rationale of the previous examples, the employee may become extremely nervous, not because of the prospect of extra work, but of what the task means. If he is doing something dumb — and winners don't do dumb things — he can't be a winner. Based on a scrap of evidence, he feels like he has a large "L" glued to his forehead. The employee doesn't fully understand why he is angry about something so small, but, regardless, he loses his temper.

Finally for this section, sometimes highly successful humans, like wealthy executives or world champion athletes, suffer a rare defeat which causes them to jump directly to the Loser Drawer — without 'passing go' — leaving them devastated. Like the prisoner in the squalid prison, a one-off failure can cause him to be reclassified from 'hero to zero' in an instant.

We know it is difficult to believe things can get so intense, so to illustrate our point further, here's a situation we once witnessed on Earth. There was a world-champion female fighter, undefeated throughout her career, whom we will call Rosa Reyna. With such a glowing resume, you would think that nothing could rattle this fighter, right? Well, unbelievably, she considered committing suicide after the inevitable happened: She finally suffered a defeat. We repeat, after the first loss in her career — a record no other human had achieved at that time — she contemplated suicide.

So, it's not only regular humans who are prone to extreme reactions, but also the *crème de la crème* — the elite. Rosa Reyna, after facing one 'bump in the road', felt so devastated that she considered killing herself. And it's worth pointing out that despite her defeat, while she thought of suicide, she was still considered the greatest female fighter of all time.

Do you get the picture? Can you see how destructive having too few Drawers can be? Even for the most advanced human specimens, the effects can be devastating. Now, imagine regular humans, the ones you will usually hunt. How easy can it get?

There are other famous cases with executives and sportspeople. Of course, not all reach the point of wanting to blow out their brains, but you wouldn't believe how often outwardly successful humans become disproportionately devastated by small setbacks.

By now you might be thinking, *"This is too crazy. How can I tell whether my prey has a small number of drawers and if it does, how can I use the fact against it?"*

Well, understand this: An overreaction usually indicates a small number of Drawers. You see, exaggerated emotions are often caused by extra meanings that develop because of the winner/loser way of analysing things — a small mistake meaning to a human that he is a loser. So, whenever a human overreacts to a situation, like in the Rosa Reyna example, it usually indicates that he has a poor grasp of reality and probably constantly fears becoming a loser. As a hunter, however, like with the other features, only after consistent observation must you reach conclusions about your prey — one or two isolated events aren't enough.

We will continue with several more examples and stick with the Drawer metaphor because, to be able to manipulate humans, it is crucial that you understand this concept. You may feel that the message is becoming repetitive. However, we assure you that it needs to be.

Moving on…

Drawers causing trouble in human relationships:
A human believes he will end up in the Loser Drawer if his partner has an affair. So, like a frightened animal, he is crazily insecure and obsessed with every action his partner takes. As expected, he most often has no idea about the root of his insecurity. At the Captain's level, he just knows he is obsessed with his partner.

Do you see how too few Drawers can cause problems before one even exists? If the human believes being cheated on makes him a loser, his relationship will be like a pressure cooker — even before his partner considers giving another suiter the 'glad eye'. For this fragile creature, there's much at stake, so he lives in constant fear of betrayal — even the faintest whiff of infidelity will cause him to question the future of the relationship. To this human, it's as if an affair, or a marriage breakdown, is directly linked to a threat to his life. Can you grasp how this daily nightmare is similar to what the prisoner endures?

Here are two more examples:

One night, a male human can't 'get it up' in bed (loses his erection). This failure to perform leads him directly to the Loser Drawer. Suddenly, his manhood is under threat, so he takes refuge in denial and blame: *"It never happened! She's at fault."*

A couple has a good relationship, but after a brief period of no sex, one of them begins to believe they are in trouble; their relationship is doomed.

By the way, of course, some of these conclusions could be true — no sex could indicate cracks in a relationship. However, it can also mean many other things: There could be an issue outside the relationship or, perhaps, no problem at all. What is interesting is that when a human feels the threat of heading to the Loser Drawer, he can hardly think straight. He can't see the difference between it *can* be a problem and it *is* a problem, a small clue and a final statement.

Labelling and categorising affects humans all the time. Even a tardy response to a text message can be interpreted as a threat to a relationship or something equally ominous. Yes, humans continuously use small clues to reach far bigger conclusions. Life for them must be truly exhausting.

AS USUAL, THIS CONCEPT ALSO RUNS DEEPER...

Do you see how Drawers distort reality? Here's an example of how they work in a more complex situation that isn't easy to spot at first:

Sometimes, with a couple, the female may start to earn more money than the male, and the relationship jumps into a crisis. If you ask the male to explain the reasons for the fights and arguments, he may have clear, straightforward issues to complain about. But, only by digging deeper can you identify the real problem, which is his interpretation of the situation as "unbearable" and him labelling himself as a loser.

How come?

Well, imagine two big Drawers:

1. Winner (successful, earn more money, dominance, etc.) — a big

package.

2. Loser (everything that doesn't fit into the Winner Drawer) — another big package.

You see, on Earth, money and dominance are often placed in the same Drawer (Winner), and many male humans think they have to be dominant in a relationship. So, the rationale is that by earning less money than their partner, their dominance is threatened, which could send them to the Loser Drawer. Crazy, isn't it?

And, most incredibly, these males often freak out and, despite having strong feelings for their partners, end their relationships just to escape the situation — without understanding why they feel so threatened.

Should a 'threatened' human explain his reasons for his relationship crisis, few would question him. Sure, some advanced creatures will realise that his partner's superior earning power is probably the root of the problem. However, almost none will realise that the issue runs far deeper.

How so? Well, the real problem is the male human's low number of Drawers, his interpretation of the world and poor understanding of life's complexities. An experienced hunter would know that, for this male human, the correct remedy would be to change his definitions of money, dominance and a male's role in a relationship, and create new Drawers in between Winner and Loser. Of course, this is easier said than done.

At all times, humans label things and situations; they confuse small indicators with final statements and overrate the consequences. It is a form of cognitive bias in which the brain allows a minuscule and specific trait to influence a human's overall evaluation of another human, an object or a situation. While in prison, it is understandable that an inmate will be petrified of showing a flaw. In real life, it shouldn't be that bad. But, it can be. Pay attention to overreactions or misunderstandings; they will provide valuable clues to explore later.

***

Tip: If a human relies on small clues, you can fabricate them and let him reach the big conclusions that you want. You can create a whole new image of yourself based on minor details that are easy to arrange. So, can you fabricate small conclusion-forming clues to enthral and intimidate a human? You bet!

STRANGE HUMAN ALLERGIES

With Drawers — and the risk of being a loser — some humans develop, what we call "Allergies" to certain words or situations. Yes, you read right. We are not talking about an allergic reaction to a particular food, pollen, fur or dust; no, we mean an aversion to certain situations — even specific words. When exposed to their Allergies, humans display extreme reactions — a complete rejection of any sign of disapproval is a good example.

As you can imagine, an Allergy should be perceived as a weakness or vulnerability because the human has difficulty coping with something that is harmless to most others. For example, some humans break out in 'psychological hives' when exposed to a situation that implies they are not perfect. This kind of Allergy might seem positive and not a weakness. After all, what's wrong with being determined to avoid losing? This is not the case, though. Make no mistake: For a human, his Allergies are a nightmare, and an inability to cope with loss is different to not liking and avoiding losing. We're not talking about a creature who pursues success; no, instead, we mean one who runs from failure and can't afford to be imperfect.

Of course, to humans, striving to win or succeed in life seems like a worthwhile pursuit. And it is. However, what we're talking about is humans who dread the smallest possibility of making a mistake and being sent to the Loser Drawer. Day and night, they are tormented by the threat of not being perfect. These kind of humans, my friend, you can use.

Here's an example to clarify how serious the problem is: There are two fighters. One can cope with a few punches to the face, while the other can't deal with the slightest touch. Who do you think will win? In the same way, which prey do you think is easier to catch: one who avoids but can cope with mistakes or another who freaks out with the smallest flaw?

An Allergy is a condition, an illness. It is a nightmare similar to that experienced by the prisoner who can't display any weaknesses for fear of death. Some humans can't cope with any loss — even losing a friendly game of soccer or being rejected by a member of the opposite sex can be too much to bear.

For most humans, Allergies are based on insecurity, uncontrollable emotions or needs. Identify a human's Allergies, and you can control him. In other words, determine the source of your human prey's aversion to a situation or word, etc., and use it to manipulate him.

Also, understand that if a human is extremely upset after a small mistake, it is usually because, in his mind, he has jumped from the Winner to Loser Drawer. This creature probably has an Allergy to mistakes and is terrified of committing one. Think about the student whose class presentation will label him as either a success or failure.

CURIOSITY: DRAWERS, WEAK CAPTAIN & REPETITION

Sure, a small mistake isn't usually enough to consider a human a loser or easy prey. Fair enough. However, if a human continually fails at his job, he probably *is* a loser in that part of his life, wouldn't you say? And, one would think this creature should recognise the fact immediately and take action by either upskilling or accepting that he sucks at his current occupation and should move on. However, as you now are aware, in the minds of most humans, there are usually just two Drawers, so they can't accept that they are not good at something and should try something else — they will become a loser! It's like they are failures at everything when that's unquestionably not the case. Consequently, humans ignore problems, using the Weak Captain's strategies of blame and denial. Yes, these animals often deny reality because accepting they are a loser in one aspect of their life is too painful. To them, being a failure in one thing and an achiever in another isn't possible. Blame and denial never fix the problems humans face, so they experience them over and over — it's a never-ending cycle.

AVOID CREATURES WITH MANY DRAWERS

One way to explain our point is to compare some extreme situations. Of course, the absolute opposite of the humans described so far are those with many Drawers. These more balanced creatures don't sway between the extremes of winner and loser because they have multiple places to categorise information.

Furnished with multiple drawers, these creatures would be able to cope with the fact that, just like pigs suck at flying, they can't be good at everything, a reality that humans with few Drawers can't handle.

In an ideal world (for your prey, that is), all humans would have one Drawer for every situation or human at any particular time. Then, they would see the 'real reality' around them. Having an almost limitless number of Drawers inside their heads, however, makes information storage complex and requires lots of energy, time and reflection, which is all too hard for most humans.

Let's check out how these two types of humans, Duel- and Multiple-Drawer, perceive different realities:

More than once we have observed certain humans stating, supported by research, that particular ethnic groups commit more crime than others.

A human with multiple Drawers probably wouldn't consign such a speaker to either the Good or Bad Drawer. He has many categories and would most likely understand that the speaker doesn't necessarily mean that he believes the group is inferior to others. Consequently, the Multi-Drawer human would sit through the speaker's speech and learn, for example, that the conclusions of the research could be due to economic, cultural or historical reasons — not the DNA of the ethnic group in question. He would understand that the speaker stated the facts to call attention to the problem; he was trying to help, not condemn, this group of humans.

How do you think a human with duel Drawers might react?

How about this? After listening to the speaker's opening sentence, a human with few Drawers would probably place him in the Bad Drawer (racist, bad, etc.). Then, he would refute anything the speaker says. No discussion would take place.

You see, for this Duel-Drawer human, the facts don't matter; he won't listen. Why? Well, he can't cope with conflicting or complex ideas — he lacks the Drawers to accommodate them. The rationale seems to be, *"Why is he saying that about this ethnic group? He must hate them and think they are inferior."* Got it? Inside this human's brain, the Messenger can only choose between two available Drawers, so he places the speaker in the one for enemies.

Interestingly, in this case, both the Duel- and Multi-Drawer humans — as well as the speaker — want the same thing: to help the ethnic group. But the Duel-Drawer human argues with the speaker because he can't process conflicting data and so places the speaker into the Bad Drawer.

The same thing happens in other situations, such as when a right-wing politician proposes something (like tax reform or a subsidy for a certain sector) that left-wing voters almost completely agree with, but because they are listening to the 'enemy', they attack all aspects of the proposal. After all, how could they possibly agree with a right-wing politician? Bizarre.

Complex information is difficult to process. So, it's easier for humans to simplify things by working with big categories — Drawers with many meanings — than to analyse it separately. And huge categories often distort reality. If you're not convinced, observe Earth's smartest primates discussing politics and who they will vote for. Honestly, watching them blame and deny is hilarious.

Lastly, don't worry: Almost all humans are miles away from having multiple Drawers. You see, while having many categories to better understand reality makes sense, getting them isn't easy, and almost no humans reach that stage.

TO CONCLUDE

Some hunters confuse Drawers and Hidden Associations. To make things clear, the Drawers in a human's mind multiply problems that begin with meanings.

When you observe your prey presenting abnormal behaviour, you should always ask:

- *What does it mean to this animal?*
- *Can it differentiate between assumptions and facts?*
- *How does it categorise a situation?*
- *Does this animal have only a few Drawers, or does it have more?*

From a hunter's perspective, the fewer Drawers a human has the better, because fewer Drawers cause extreme behaviours. It can be tricky to conclude why a human behaves strangely at first, so you must pay close attention because not even humans are aware of why they react in certain ways.

Do you want to hear a joke? Despite not knowing themselves (how their mind works, their crazy Hidden Associations and Drawers), humans usually demand that their friends, family and partners understand them, and they get angry if they don't. Haha!

In Part III, we explain how humans' bodies translate everything discussed in this chapter. We also explore the role of human emotions and desires.

PART III
BETWEEN
REALITIES & DESIRES

8

THE BRAIN'S PUPPET
EMOTIONS & DESIRES

Now we will explain how a human becomes his Brain's Puppet.

<u>Note</u>: Because the ideas in this chapter apply to all the others, we have kept it brief. Keep this concept in mind while reading Part IV: *What drives the animal.*

THE MECHANISM

We'll use two simple examples: one of an ancient sage and the other related to dog training.

<u>Tell a human this story: The ancient sage</u>
> *Imagine a human who, without question, follows all advice, suggestions and demands of a 200-year-old blind sage who is ignorant about technology and modern life. No matter what, at all times, the human obediently follows.*

<u>How does this example apply to humans? And how can you use it against them?</u>

Any human would say it is wise to listen and learn from those who are more experienced. But they would also say that the example above makes no sense because this sage is out of touch and bound to give poor advice. So, it would make sense to listen but, at the same time, question any advice he provides.

Fair enough, no?

However, what happens in the example above is similar to what humans do when their brains instruct them, by way of emotions and desires, to do something. That's right, the (ancient) brain, which developed several thousand years ago, and doesn't understand modern life or technology, calls the shots. And, without question, humans follow orders. So, if the brain instructs to be scared, angry, or anything else, the 'puppet' obediently follows its 'wise' central system.

When the Messenger (or brain) detects a potentially threatening pattern, it switches to war mode. The human, though, might only be preparing for a class presentation, as explained in the *Human Drawers* chapter. For you, the hunter, this mismatch opens up opportunities.

So, emotions play a crucial role in how humans behave, and humans are hardly able to question them. And, of course, the brain's signals (emotions) are not always right.

Check out this second example, and then we will jump to explanations.

<u>Dog training:</u>

Now, if you talk to humans about dog training, almost all will be familiar with the system of pleasure and pain, a simple method for reinforcing behaviour that the trainer wants and discouraging behaviour he doesn't want. Humans know that to train a dog, they should give it a treat when it does something right and punish it when it does something wrong. As time goes by, the animal will learn to behave and do whatever the human wants. Simple.

For humans, this is obvious but would probably be a complete surprise (if it were possible to explain) to the dog. It's safe to assume that the animal won't understand the method being used to manipulate it.

However, should you confront a human with the fact that his brain has been training him, and at a much larger scale (24 hours a day since birth), he will probably enter into, what we call, "denial mode".

<u>Linking the ancient sage & dog training:</u>
Humans struggle enormously to understand that what they feel is not necessarily right, wrong, or, in fact, anything at all. It is merely good or bad stuff that their central system uses to train and guide them. So, just like 'Fido', most humans have limited self-understanding — they are their Brain's Puppets.

The previous examples show that the brain uses a human's emotions to guide him to do what it believes is best — from avoiding pain, to seeking pleasure and feeling good about it.

The truth is that the human brain applies the same technique as a dog trainer; it reinforces good stuff with pleasure and the bad with pain. And, as one can expect, pain can be extremely persuasive. Ask a human if he would brush his teeth more often if failing to do so hurt.

The human brain, though, was designed thousands of years ago for animals clinging to survival in the jungle. Consequently, it still reinforces unnecessary behaviours — overeating sugar or fat, for example. Again, if a certain level of sugar started to hurt, humans would soon stop munching on sugary treats. You can bet on it.

Anyway, the essential thing to remember is that a human's brain has been training him since birth, so most humans, like obedient dogs, are unaware of why they like some things and dislike others.

The same happens when humans are angry, nervous, scared, happy or in love, etc. These feelings are signals from the brain, and at times they are misleading due to the limitations already discussed. After all, keep in mind that the ancient sage isn't always right — even though he has been around for many years.

Consequently, a human can consume extreme levels of fat or sugar, become irate with an inattentive waiter and fear losing things he doesn't need — losing something feels like going to the Loser Drawer. Or, a human can even love an abusive partner because he feels familiar. The list goes on and on.

CLOSE TO TOTAL CONTROL

So, the ancient sage inside a human's head is extremely powerful, don't you agree? Check out this:

As you saw at the beginning of this book, the human brain (the Messenger) creates reality, with some editing, based on what it wants the Captain to see.

And, as if that's not enough, the brain, training him like a puppet, also decides when to send a human pleasant or unpleasant messages.

That's a lot of control. One could say it's about time the Captain stopped trusting his Messenger so much and started asking questions.

DESIRES, TOO, CAN BE MISLEADING

Misleading desires are tricky for humans to understand. In the chapter *Hidden Associations* we explained that a human who expresses a desire to own a business, to become an entrepreneur, might actually long for freedom and recognition, not actually having a business.

Humans, most often, don't really understand the real reasons for their desires. Like in the example above, when stalking your prey, it's important to understand why it longs for freedom. Perhaps it has a terrible boss and feels pressured? Anyway, what matters is that if this human understood what he seeks is freedom and recognition, he could find plenty of easier ways to get those things than starting a business, which might not match his personality. Maybe the human should just change jobs, for example. But humans most often don't fully understand their desires and just follow what their brains think they need.

Remember the obedient human (good student) who falls in love with the troubled student because of a desire to feel independent and mature? Of course, there could also be other reasons, but what matters is that humans don't question or understand their desires. If the good student knew that, deep down, she sought independence and maturity, she would look at other ways of getting them.

Do you see how the human brain implants desires to get what it feels is needed? And how humans are often just puppets?

We address how the brain decides what it wants in Part IV: *What drives the animal*. For now, though, just keep in mind that humans rarely question assumptions that translate into desires and emotions — they feel too real.

The next case is a real situation that we have observed. We warn you that even for experienced hunters, it seems odd and, so, is hard to believe.

<u>Disclaimer:</u> Before you read on, we must acknowledge that, of course, there could be MANY OTHER REASONS for the human's desire. For this example we explore ONLY ONE to show how ABSURD things can get.

<u>The hidden & unbearable competition:</u>
A human, who'd so far enjoyed a fairly successful career, moved to another city, and he had some excellent reasons to go — an amazing place, beautiful weather and beaches, etc. Later, though, after a period of observation, it became apparent to us that none of those reasons were true.

You see, in reality, the human's desire to live far away from home originated from the fact that he couldn't bear seeing his parents admire his more successful sister, even though he was unaware of the assumption his brain was making. If you were to ask him if he competes with his sister, he'd sincerely say, *"What are you talking about? Of course not!"*

You see, the human couldn't realise that he COMPETES with his sister for his parents' attention, love, or whatever you want to call it. Instead, he felt more comfortable living far from home — even though he got homesick. All the human knew was that he wanted to live far away. He recognised his desire but wasn't entirely aware of his brain's assumptions behind the scenes.

As weird as it sounds, the human's sister hadn't provoked his behaviour, nor did the 'amazing' new city. Instead, his brain's assumptions *("I need to compete and win against my sister to gain my parents' acceptance and love. I can't stand losing and being in the Loser Drawer. If I can't win, I'd better escape.")* created the desire to live away from home.

So, he didn't fully understand the reasons for his desire to live far away from home and, when asked, he would often come up with the wrong explanation. By the way, yes, this sounds absurd, but it's not uncommon.

Hidden competition happens more often on Earth than humans imagine — like between males of the same tribe (the mate and father of a female, for example) competing for dominance of the house/family. Often you can see hidden competition disguised in weird discussions and small actions.

Can you see how competition is far more prevalent in human behaviour than they can recognise and how it affects humans' emotions and desires at a much deeper level than they know?

Humans are complicated animals, aren't they? Their ridiculous Hidden Associations can create not just emotions, but also desires to instruct them to do what their brains believe they should. And, humans can make minor and major decisions about their careers, marriages, etc., while unaware of the real reasons why.

You see, like their emotions, humans usually don't fully understand their desires either, and they, like puppets, just follow what their brain thinks they need. Best of all, things aren't likely to change any time soon. We explain one of the reasons why next.

***

<u>Tip:</u> Carefully observe your human prey's desire. *"What does he long for? To live in another city? Change his job, even career?"* Try to find the root. *"Why does he desire that?"* Determine if he is, in fact, ESCAPING from something, and if so, from what; this knowledge can be a weapon for manipulation. Your prey's lack of self-understanding should make him easy to play with.

***

HUMANS' LACK OF AN OUTSIDER'S POINT OF VIEW

Humans struggle to observe themselves from the sceptical perspective of an outsider.

A lion, for example, doesn't understand or question its instincts and just follows them naturally. A human scientist, however, is able to observe the lion from an outsider's point of view, knowing the animal's behaviours.

So, humans can only question their instincts, beliefs, emotions, Hidden Associations, if they study themselves from the sceptical perspective of an outsider, like a creature from another planet. But they hardly ever do.

After all, can you imagine a human about to lose his temper and then asking, *"Why am I nervous? What does this situation mean to me? Should I feel this way? What can I learn from my nervousness? What does this desire mean to me? What I am really looking for here? Am I trying to escape from something?"*

Can you imagine a human questioning his emotions or desires this way? No, right?

It is beyond most humans' capacity to study their emotions sceptically as if from outside their bodies.

Imagine a human who has never left his country. He would find it nearly impossible to question his culture, rituals (weddings, funerals, human greetings, etc.), expected social behaviours, social structures and religious beliefs.

For this human, given that he has known no other life, everything seems natural and as it should be. How could he possibly feel otherwise? Meanwhile, a foreigner would have a very different perspective and be able to evaluate these things from an outsider's perspective.

So, humans would enjoy enormous benefits if it were possible to observe themselves through the eyes of a sceptical outsider, an alien that was able to question their beliefs, emotions, desires and reality.

For most humans, however, seeing their lives from the outside is almost impossible. Consequently, they can't understand themselves or question their emotions and desires. So, as we've mentioned before, things aren't likely to change any time soon

CONCLUSIONS

Emotions play a crucial role in how humans behave, and, like their Brain's Puppets, they don't usually question them. Of course, signals from the brain are not always correct, as you have seen on pretty much every page of this book.

Also, due to humans' lack of an outsider's point of view, it is almost impossible for them to realise that they should question their emotions.

So, they become the obedient puppets of an ancient central system designed for the jungle.

What you have learned so far regarding humans' emotions and desires will be crucial for understanding Part IV where we look at the things that drive humans: vanity, Expanded Self-Interest and fear.

So, over the following chapters, keep in mind that Earth's smartest primate has such a poor understanding of its emotions and desires that it, for example, also completely misunderstands Self-Interest, which is rather interesting.

PART IV
WHAT DRIVES THE ANIMAL

9

PRELUDE TO THE CHAPTER 'PERSONAL HOLY GRAIL'
PERCEIVED LACK OF POWER

Following on from the previous chapter, and before we address the concept of a human's Holy Grail, we must explain one of the things that makes humans feel good or bad, powerful or powerless, superior or inferior, in or out of control. Doing so will help you understand how vanity, which we address in the next chapter, works.

In this prelude, you will see that humans become angry or irritated (or simply feel unpleasant sensations) when they perceive that they can't do what they need or want. You will see that when humans feel powerless, they get unpleasant sensations, and, conversely, when they get what they want, they feel in control and powerful — all pleasant sensations.

Interestingly, when a human becomes angry in his day-to-day life, he usually can't see that the real source of his ire is his PERCEIVED LACK OF POWER or control over a situation.

If things are not clear yet, don't you worry. It is possible to create artificial situations to demonstrate the link between irritability and a perceived lack of power.

AN EXPERIMENT: ARTIFICIALLY CREATING FEELINGS OF POWERLESSNESS WITHIN THE HUMAN MIND

Most humans like to have a minimum amount of control over their surroundings. So, you can expose your prey to situations he can't control and then revel in seeing him experience unpleasant sensations.

For example, ask a human to help you with something like driving lessons. Then, pretend to be a terrible learner who can't follow instructions.

He will say things like *"Turn. I said turn. Hey! Turn, man! You missed the turn-off!"* Watch the human's demeanour shift as you fail to follow his instructions, not because you can't, but because he believes you can't. In situations like this, after a few minutes, the human will usually feel discomfort and probably hate being unable to get you, the learner, to do what he wants (turn, stop or park). The human may keep cool at the beginning, but, as time goes by, he will usually become angry.

What have you observed?

Naturally, the human will slowly realise that he isn't powerful enough to change what's happening. And his ancient brain hates not being in control, even in a safe situation like a driving lesson. That's just how the brain operates. So, it will send requests (emotions) for the human to do something about the situation, unpleasant sensations to get him out of the car, or take control, etc. The source of the problem, as usual, is the perceived lack of control over a situation. Even if it doesn't matter much.

Here's a more straightforward example: Let a human play a video game with controls that don't work properly. The human will, understandably, feel uncomfortable due to his inability to do what he wants to in the situation.

You see, humans feel good and more powerful when they can do or get what they want, and they feel the opposite when they can't. The idea is so simple that we can test it by artificially creating an irritating experience. Easy.

Let's look at the relationship humans have with power within their heads.

PULLING STRINGS OF POWER INSIDE THE CAPTAIN'S CABIN

Yes, we will focus on the SENSATION of lacking power, not the REALITY. Remember, the feeling of powerlessness happens inside a human's head. And, that's what interests us.

The difference in perceived and actual powerlessness may seem small. However, you will see how much easier it becomes to manipulate your prey when you understand the difference. PERCEIVED lack of power or control is more important than reality because humans can perceive powerlessness in situations that aren't so obvious.

Remember the human who became irritated simply because another human ignored his advice? Like in that scenario, there are many situations where nothing much happens in the real world, but, regardless, a human perceives a lack of power to do what he wants. And the feeling is often strong enough to irritate him.

Okay. But, what are we trying to say?

You see, from this perspective, a human who feels unpleasant sensations caused by a disrespectful boss, in fact, feels this way because he perceives a lack of power to fix the situation. So, the terrible boss is not the source of the problem; he just exposes it. The cause could be, for example, the human's perceived incapacity to find another job, which obligates him to stay with this boss. Yes, the cause, most often, is a perceived weakness or insecurity that was already there. Otherwise, a disrespectful boss wouldn't bother him; after all, he would be able to walk away at any time.

***

Again, this is crucial: The cause of a human's ire is his perceived weakness or insecurity which the problem exposes.

***

So, PERCEIVED lack of power or control is more important than what is actually happening outside due to the crazy reality the Captain can perceive from within the Cabin.

Interestingly, it's not so easy to observe human behaviours and reach conclusions quickly. A distracted hunter can get things wrong, as you will see.

WARNING:
COMPENSATORY BEHAVIOUR CAN BE MISLEADING

Here, also, you must be very careful in your analysis because, as usual, the concept goes deep, and a careless observation can lead to wrong conclusions.

Humans try to balance a minimum amount of perceived power (pleasant sensations) in their minds. As we said, lacking power is unpleasant for humans, and sometimes they compensate for the discomfort by acquiring short-term pleasure or power from other things.

For example, a human gets dumped (an unwanted divorce), so he indulges in compulsive shopping to compensate. Or, a human loses his job and kicks someone's arse in a bar to make himself feel powerful again.

You see, in both situations, each human is trying to re-establish a perceived minimum level of power and pleasure.

With these humans, you may judge them based on their actions in the shopping centre or bar. However, doing so will lead you to false conclusions about the reasons for their behaviour. If you fail to dig deeply enough, you might not get the full picture.

To reach an accurate conclusion about your prey, take time for deep analysis. If you observe long enough, often you will discover that the root of the problem is some dissatisfaction that was there before the act that exposes it.

Note: In the case of the brawling human, it's quite funny because other animals usually fight for food (hunt), or to reproduce, which are final and straightforward goals. With humans, though, the reasons for fighting are often obscured and not what they appear. Instead, engaging in 'fisticuffs' is often the result of another frustration or disappointment that stems from a Hidden Association, as you have already seen.

TAKEAWAYS FROM THIS PRELUDE

As you know, everything happens inside the human's head, and the

Brain's Puppet concept is everywhere.

The human brain hates perceiving a lack of power or control over a situation, and so, when it feels power or control is lacking, it sends unpleasant sensations to make the human react.

PERCEIVED is the key word in our analysis because the feeling of powerlessness happens inside a human's head.

Remember: Humans are complex animals, and what can appear to be the cause of a problem can, in fact, just be exposing it (like the human fighting in a bar due to problems that happened before he arrived for a drink). So, be careful before you reach conclusions.

This may all sound confusing. Don't worry; everything will fall into place in the next chapter when we explore the concept in more detail. For now, what matters is that you get the general idea.

It is important to note, though, that each prey wants and needs to control different things and at different levels, depending on many things — we will explore in the next chapter. Just keep the concept of perceived lack of power fresh in your mind.

So, now with our intro complete, it is time to play with a human's vanity — that's what the Personal Holy Grail is primarily about.

10

PERSONAL HOLY GRAIL
VANITY

In a war, knowing your enemy's next move provides an enormous advantage. It's the same when hunting humans — you must know where they are heading so you can set traps in the right places.

But, how can you know a human's destination? Well, pay attention to what he is proud of — his vanity, what he admires. These are what guide his decisions and noticing them will enable you to know what he will do next.

You see, though rarely clear in their minds (at the Captain's level), each human pursues a goal, a mission, a quest. We call it a "Personal Holy Grail". If you can identify your prey's Holy Grail, you will gain a considerable advantage, especially as humans themselves usually don't know what it is. At least their Captains don't. They are, you could say, most often in the dark.

We know this may all sound ludicrous — even contradictory. How can a human chase something unknowingly? We will explain. For now, though, keep in mind that a human's Captain is NOT always aware of the goals he chases.

If you identify a human's self-image, which summarises whom he wishes to be, his admiration, his vanity, what he is proud of, you will know where he is heading — better than himself. If you do this, your prey will become predictable, and you will know, with confidence, where to set a trap and which bait to use.

While this concept may sound abstract, things will become clearer. Wait and see. In this chapter, you will learn an easy-to-understand method for playing with your human prey's vanity.

DISCLAIMER:
OVER THE FOLLOWING PAGES, NO FAITH IS NECESSARY

Before we begin, let's be crystal clear here. We will NOT abandon our strictly sceptical-hunter point of view. The idea we are about to explain is a simplification and might sound absurd. Of course, the concept of a Personal Holy Grail is not literal, but it summaries vanity, Hidden Associations and Drawers, etc. simply, and you will find it highly useful for understanding how humans' vanity is central in their lives.

The Holy Grail concept also helps explain a human's Expanded Self-Interest, which we cover in the next chapter.

THE LINK BETWEEN THE PRELUDE & THIS CHAPTER

In the prelude to this chapter, we explained that:

- Everything happens inside humans' minds. Consequently, how they PERCEIVE a situation is crucial.
- Humans hate perceiving that they lack power to do what they want (or need) to do. They hate the feeling of not being in control of a thing or situation.

Quite obvious, simple and easy.

Now we will analyse what happens inside humans' heads in more common (less extreme) situations, not ones that involve intense emotions (fear, hate, anger, etc.) due to the animal's perceived lack of power or control. Yes, we will focus on when a human perceives slightly less power than he thought he had, that he is a little farther from the level of control he wants. Of course, we'll also look at the opposite — when he feels a bit more powerful, in control and closer to where he wants to be.

So, how does it all work?

THE QUEST INSIDE EVERY HUMAN

<u>Tell a human this story: The mission</u>

Consider the same captain and ancient ship discussed in previous chapters. Now, imagine that the captain, the messenger and the crew, based on past experiences, have beliefs about which island to sail towards to feel safe. The safe island is the ship's mission.

It's easy to imagine that if an enemy knows where the ship is, and to which island it is sailing, it shouldn't be difficult to stay ahead and prepare an ambush at the right time and place. So, knowing the route, which is the line between the ship and its goal, provides a significant advantage to the enemy. We call this line the "Line of Power".

Note that with this Line of Power, whenever the captain and crew feel they are heading in the right direction, they feel good, excited, and, as the name suggests, more powerful. However, whenever they think they are travelling in the wrong direction — even backwards — the captain and crew feel bad or less powerful and all because they are farther from their goal. Obviously, any event or obstacle that doesn't fall onto the line is irrelevant.

So, in summary, the ship has a mission, and it is possible to draw a path, a route, a line, between the ship and its final goal. The captain's decisions are related to this Line of Power; when the vessel is closer to the ultimate goal, the captain and crew feel good; farther away, they feel bad.

<u>How does this apply to humans? And how can you use it against them?</u>
Well, humans work pretty much the same way as the captain and crew on a ship.

To simplify several concepts, let's say that each human also has a Line of Power. This line traverses between whom the human thinks he is (his self-image) and whom he wants to be.

By whom he wants to be, we mean a super version of himself, of what he is on a quest to become. Like the Crusaders of old, every human seeks a Personal Holy Grail — a dream, a super-self, a goal.

So, there is the Line of Power that is the route to reach the Holy Grail. Just like a ship on a mission, humans feel good when they perceive they are getting closer to their Holy Grail and bad when they perceive they are slipping farther away. Simple.

Let's explore these two concepts and then see how they fit together. And, of course, how you can use them against humans during a hunt.

THE LINE OF POWER

This Line of Power concept is pretty straightforward, so we will pass by it quickly. The tricky part is the Holy Grail.

As mentioned, the Line of Power is the rope that links a human's current self-image to his Holy Grail.

But, make no mistake: Although a simple concept, recognising your prey's Line of Power is essential for knowing where to attack later.

Why? Well, because, in general, only things that relate to a human's Line of Power will affect him. Events outside it will usually have little or no impact. To attack things that fall outside a human's Line of Power is like, using the ship as an example, placing obstacles and preparing an ambush in places beyond the ship's route.

A human, say, can believe he is becoming skilled at something, and a mistake shows he isn't as good as he thought. So, his brain sends him a bad feeling. Simple. However, errors that are unrelated to what a human wants won't affect him. For example, losing a sporting match or some money — even a marriage — can have little or no effect if the human's dream is based almost entirely on becoming a great writer. Point out a small mistake in his prose, though, and watch him try to stab you with his 'poison pen'. You will become a threat. Again, other mistakes won't have much bearing on his self-image and won't block his route to what he wants to be, but a small writing error could. So, this is why humans become angry when they make mistakes while doing things that matter to them.

Yes, it is obvious that events outside a human's Line of Power will have no effect, but, as you will see, humans usually don't understand this fact.

Okay, let's dig deeper into the concept that all humans pursue a Personal Holy Grail, and let's also explain how you can use it against them.

A HUMAN'S PERSONAL HOLY GRAIL

A human's Personal Holy Grail usually depends on a combination of traits: his beliefs, knowledge and past experiences (especially childhood), for example. It is the product of his desire to feel happier, safer and more accepted, etc.

The Holy Grail is more complicated than you might expect. Let's look at it in more detail: To build a super version of himself in his mind, a human considers his capabilities, passions and what wins him social approval. His friends, parents and society have a significant influence. A human's super-self could include components of what his parents taught him, what he admires in others and what his society promotes — as well as what he believes will be in his best interests. All these create the image of what would be a winner for him.

As you can see, many things influence the formation of a human's Holy Grail. And, as if this isn't enough, Hidden Associations and Drawers in a human's mind have significant sway over his perception of how to become a winner.

Keep in mind that, as mentioned, a human's super-self is our primary consideration when discussing his goal; it is imperative. But, at times, the situation he desires, the places he wants to go to, the people he wants by his side, also have an influence.

Regardless of what a human's goal is, it is the result of all we have mentioned. His super-self is the consequence of what his Captain and Crew want — things he is aware of as well as suppressed memories that only in-depth inner investigation can bring to the surface. The result is an image of the best a human believes he can become. His Personal Holy Grail.

The tricky part is that assumptions behind humans' conclusions vary widely based on everything that influences their decisions. So, each prey's super-self can differ wildly.

A human's ideal could be, for example, to become incredibly wealthy, beautiful, or to be a nice person whom everybody loves. It could also be to become omnipotent — even a terrorist or drug lord.

Yes, some humans aspire to do what they call "evil". One can dream of studying to become a doctor and save lives while another can aspire to becoming a terrorist and committing mass murder. As strange as it sounds, a human forms his super-self (doctor or terrorist) based on what he believes is best for him, on what he admires. So, whether a doctor or terrorist, at a deep level, both humans chase the same thing — their super-self.

Or, a human can be proud of being the 'smart guy' — the 'shyster' who earns the most money with the least amount of work, regardless of whether or not he did the right thing. Why should he care?

So, you see that humans can have goals that are useful to society and ones that are detrimental. We prefer not to label goals "good" or "bad". Whatever a human's purpose is (Holy Grail), what matters to him is whether he is getting closer to or farther away from it. And, we must point out that once a human has consolidated a goal, it is difficult to change his focus. For example, you'd have a hard time convincing a human who is proud of being a thief or terrorist to aspire to become a doctor and save lives. Changing a human's Holy Grail, would take lots of convincing because it is based on so many things, including, as we said, suppressed memories.

For you, this is okay; you just need to use a human's goal for your benefit so that you know where to set a trap and how to manipulate him.

A human's Personal Holy Grail is the product of his definition of success.

SO...WHAT IS SUCCESS?

The accomplishment of something (a purpose, a dream) is a simple definition of success, according to the human 'code'. *Success*. It is just one word. However, look deeper, and you will see that its meaning carries a lot; every human's idea of success differs.

To illustrate the wide variety of meanings of success for humans, we have gathered several more common definitions. You see, for a human, success could mean:

- being rich and powerful and able to control everything around him (a successful entrepreneur or a drug lord, for example)
- having many sexual conquests
- being highly recognised among peers for abilities and

achievements (a professor, scientist, artist, writer, doctor — even a hacker)

- achieving a deep level of self-understanding, self-knowledge
- becoming famous and being idolised and able to influence many people
- having plenty of free time for work-life balance (fewer hours a day to earn money, but enough time to spend with family and friends)
- having no responsibility (a gypsy, for example)
- being a great son, daughter, husband, wife or parent
- having many children
- being attractive
- being married, regardless of how good the marriage is
- needing few material things (a minimalist)
- committing suicide in a terrorist attack and entering the gates of heaven in the name of God
- being able to pursue a passion (a poor, but a happy artist, for example)
- being able to change thousands of lives with a job (like working for some NGO).

The possibilities are endless!

So, as you can imagine, a wealthy executive with one child, a caveman with no money and ten children and an 18-year-old suicide bomber will all have widely opposing ideas about success. Were they to meet, it is unlikely they would understand that each considers himself successful.

Interestingly, humans usually say they understand the different definitions of success, but they have enormous difficulty understanding a human that contradicts their own.

When you identify your prey's definition of success, the Holy Grail it pursues, it is easy to understand — even predict — its reactions to particular problems.

And, to avoid any doubt, let's make it crystal clear how important this concept is. Apart from when humans are desperately in fear and trying to survive (which we cover in the chapter *Survival Mode*), almost all decisions humans make are based on their perceived super-self. If you know what a human admires — what he wants to be, his ideal image — you will have a considerable advantage.

And, in case you are wondering, there isn't much point in asking a human to explain his super-self; he will usually say whatever will gain him social acceptance — whatever he is expected to say. At the Captain's level a human rarely has a clear image of what he is trying to pursue, his definition of success — even though he is chasing it. This ignorance could be because it is too difficult to come up with the right super-self — to fully interact with his Crew, to decode the meanings and Drawers in his mind. So, as usual, you must rely on paying attention to the tips your prey provides: their words, attitudes, behaviours, reactions — recurring problems.

Let's look at some examples of reactions based on different super-selves to begin applying the concept.

QUICK, APPLIED EXAMPLES OF DIFFERENT HOLY GRAILS

Not surprisingly, individual Holy Grails cause different reactions for humans facing the same problems. Check out these examples:

When two humans are in the process of getting a divorce, the consequences of the failed relationship can be different for each partner. The male with a quest that considers only his career and money, for example, may be primarily annoyed about the financial cost; for him, this 'bump in the road' is getting in the way of his goal of financial success. The female, however, may be devastated; for her, a husband and children form her Holy Grail (a great wife and mum), the meaning of her existence. While for the male, divorce is a problem, but just a small hiccup, for the female, it is a massive rock landing on her Line of Power and impeding her mission.

Humans often think that one is more robust than the other. In fact, each just has different super-selves and so react differently to various forms of adversity. For one, a setback is a massive blow, but for the other, it's not. As simple as that.

Maybe, for the husband a setback that would match the devastation felt by his wife during a divorce would be the loss of his career, resulting in an enormous financial blow. In this case, he could be distraught, while his wife may calmly support him — even though the financial setback would be the same for both of them.

In another example, a student wants to make his parents proud of him, so he feels good when he attends school, pays attention and achieves good grades. Another student, though, can be proud of the opposite; he may believe that 'winners' don't abide by academic structure and rules. So, he creates a mission for himself: the 'smart guy' who gets by with minimal effort.

As expected, poor grades will affect each student differently, and, naturally, each will have a different reaction towards the (apparently) same regretful situation of failing an exam. For the second student, bad grades won't bother him much, and rules will hardly change his behaviour.

LAWS, RULES & ETHICS
Just obstacles

It is important to point out that laws, rules and ethics only influence the formation of a human's Personal Holy Grail, the best version of himself that will gain him more social acceptance and success, etc. But, once a human has formed his Holy Grail, rules mostly become just obstacles.

Laws and rules rarely prevent humans from trying to achieve what they believe is best for them. Think of a human who truly admires and wants to become a drug lord — a criminal who is proud of his actions. For him, the law represents merely an obstacle. In his analysis, doing wrong is still the best path to take.

We will continue to discuss humans' Holy Grails, but, first, let's look at how (inside their minds) humans continuously analyse situations to see if they are getting closer to or farther from where they want to be.

ANALYSING THE LINE OF POWER

The following diagram summarises how the Holy Grail and Line of Power work. It shows the Holy Grail (super-self) as a GOAL that defines the direction, and the Line of Power is the link, the route.

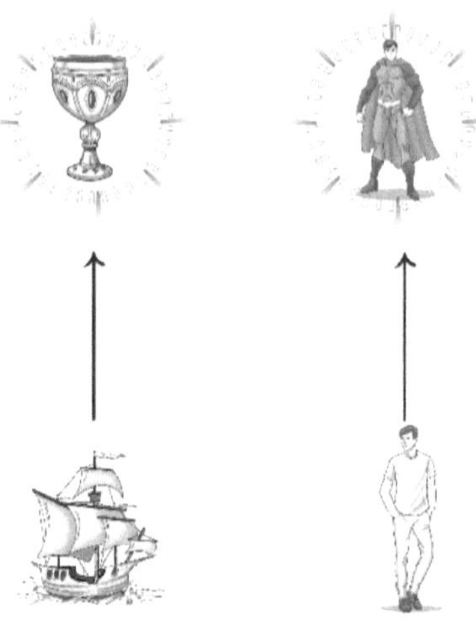

Figure 1. A representation of how the Holy Grail and the Line of Power relate to humans.

So, it is simple: closer feels good; farther away feels bad. Easy. And, of course, not much happens if there is no movement forwards or backwards.

Yes, the idea is pretty basic, but we need to state it clearly because, as a hunter, you can't afford not to have this idea set in your mind.

Also, note that humans can be more or less sensitive to the unpleasant sensations of getting farther away from their Holy Grail depending on their situation, as you will see in a later chapter. For now, keep in mind that while some humans can't cope with the slightest unpleasant sensation, others can. However, the diagram above applies to all of them.

IT'S THE DIRECTION, STUPID!

Yes, it is true that the Holy Grail represents the GOAL. However, its primary influence on a human is the DIRECTION he takes, what he is proud of and his vanity. What matters is where the Holy Grail points the human to go, not how far away it is.

As a consequence, the Holy Grail can be very distant (like wanting to change the world). The human doesn't have to accomplish his goal completely. The Holy Grail is a 'beacon' to travel towards. It defines what drives a human, what gives him pleasure or pain. So, The Holy Grail naturally guides a human's decisions.

So, let's make it clear: No matter how big the dream or how distant the Holy Grail, what matters to a human is whether or not he is moving towards it. Simple.

<u>Clarification: It is not about *wanting* less</u>

While hunting on Earth, you may hear humans discussing how better to handle dreams and expectations. You may feel that what they say is relevant to this chapter. Check out what some say: *"Expect less, and you increase your happiness."* That sounds reasonable, doesn't it? It seems kind of similar to what we are explaining, don't you agree?

Make no mistake, though. This is NOT what we mean when explaining a human's Holy Grail. Our experience shows that a human can desire whatever he wants, and his desire will define the DIRECTION he wishes to go. Sayings like *"expect less, and you increase your happiness"*, though, are only useful for the weak and spoiled — humans who can't cope with not achieving their goals, who can't handle disappointment. So, expecting less to increase happiness isn't related to our concept of the Holy Grail. Humans don't need an easy-to-reach super-self (simple and close) to enjoy pleasant sensations. However, we can use their erroneous sentence and attitude to explain a bit more about the concept of the Holy Grail.

What the phrase could say is *"NEED less, and increase your happiness"*, which is entirely different.

It's not smart for any human to NEED a lot because doing so makes it easy for others to play with his fear, as you will see later in this book. After all, when an animal lacks something it needs, like food or air, it's in trouble. However, what an animal wants is just a direction, and so can be as large as its imagination, so long as the want isn't necessary for feeling safe. Do you get the difference?

Need and Want. These two words may look similar, but they are miles apart. It is also interesting to keep in mind that often humans confuse wanting a lot with needing a lot. They paint their dreams, their Holy Grail, as a necessity. Consequently, they start NEEDING, and that's when they can't cope with disappointments. When this happens, you have an opportunity to play with fear, and there are many ways to do that, which is why we have dedicated two chapters to the subject.

Now, let's look at some manipulation tactics.

INTIMIDATE OR ENTHRAL

You can manipulate a human by creating the right threat of punishment, or by enthralling him with the right promise of reward. In other words, you can intimidate by obstructing a human's quest for the Holy Grail, or you can enthral him by playing with his vanity. Both methods will enable you to shepherd your prey to where you want it.

Just keep in mind that your actions must relate to a human's Holy Grail and Line of Power to be effective. For example, criticising the inferior grades of a student who does not care about school, or promising more money to a worker who craves free time (work-life balance) with his family, is usually pointless.

So, if you choose to threaten a human, you must know what will impede his journey towards his goal. You might attack or question his wealth, marriage, abilities or social recognition, depending on his Holy Grail. Yes, sometimes challenging some of these things can do the trick.

Also, if you choose to deceive or enthral a human to help him feel that his prize (Holy Grail) is in sight, you can do this by supporting him (or, promising support, which is easier), or by merely complimenting him on anything related to his mission.

This hapless human will often melt in your arms if you say the right words at the right time. Exalting a human's wealth and achievements can help in some cases. Commenting on his beauty or intelligence or parenting skills will work, too. It all depends on what the human is proud of.

So, it is essential to identify your prey's goals to know what to compliment and what not to criticise.

On the other hand, if you don't understand your prey's super-self, his decisions will most often appear unpredictable. Your actions will have little effect.

Strangely, while on Earth, you will see that many humans are ignorant of this simple rule, and, consequently, they attack things with no relevance to another human's Line of Power or Holy Grail. Trying to make a corrupt politician feel guilty about his treacherous acts, when he admires being the smart guy, not being honest, is an example. Any attempt at making him feel remorse will be futile — his Holy Grail is in the other direction, so don't waste your time. In cases like this, obstacles, like threats of punishment by law, are more effective for guiding your prey. But, as obvious as this sounds, humans continuously 'bark up the wrong tree', so to speak, when trying to influence others. Weird. What can you do?

<u>A criticism-compliment strategy:</u>
It's important to note that it's okay to criticise things that don't affect a human's mission if the criticism is for a purpose: establishing rapport to gain leverage to enthral your prey later, for example.

It's about finding the right things to criticise and compliment, an art you must master.

By criticising things that aren't related to your prey's Line of Power, you can often appear sincere without harming your relationship.

For example, if a human is proud of his sales skills, you might get away with criticising his agenda or financial-management skills while still praising his sales ability. By applying this criticism-compliment strategy, your praise may sound more sincere and, therefore, be more effective.

Be aware that there are exceptions. For example, when a human can't cope with any flaw due to his Drawers, or an Allergy to any loss or mistake. However, in general, criticising what isn't part of a human's Holy Grail only, and complimenting him to make him feel he is getting closer to reaching it, will help during your hunt.

Always remember, though, the manipulation game is dangerous. If your human prey realises that he is being 'played', there will be trouble. So, be careful. Adapt your words, but don't lie because you could sound fake. Find real stuff to criticise and compliment.

<u>Note: Your image can help:</u> It is far easier to manipulate your prey if he sees you as something related to his super-self. Why? Because he will listen more and question less if you resemble what he aspires to be. For example, a human who dreams of one day becoming successful in business is more likely to listen to and follow advice (without much

questioning) from a successful entrepreneur. So, does your human prey like money? Reveal your wealth. Does success to him mean needing few material possessions? Be humble. Is he religious…? By being a 'chameleon', you will lower your prey's defences and be better able to manipulate him. But, again, avoid lying because you'll risk getting caught. What's important is that you focus on what matters to your prey.

CAN THE HUNTER CHANGE HIS PREY'S HOLY GRAIL?

To use a somewhat macabre analogy, when chasing his super-self, a human is like a zombie in pursuit of human flesh. Don't get us wrong, he is still rational, but not as much as you'd think. Once you locate the 'flesh' he lusts for, the human will become quite predictable.

Can you do more? What if you were to change the location of the flesh? Naturally, your prey would lurch in a new direction. Sounds great, doesn't it? If you could place your human prey's vanity where you want, you could control his decisions as you please. For you, hunting would be much easier.

And, like the example of the corrupt politician mentioned before, some hunters sometimes do wonder if they can change their prey's super-self to guide it naturally towards the desired direction.

In our experience, it is possible to manipulate a human to change his Holy Grail. Although its roots (Hidden Associations) hardly change, over an extended period, as humans mature and experience life, their priorities and what they admire can alter. Consequently, humans can change parts of their Holy Grails themselves. Therefore, you can always try by slowly (over time) explaining and showing your prey that his mission is doomed and not worth pursuing.

So, yes, changing a human's Holy Grail is possible. However, keep in mind that it is extremely difficult to do so. Why? Well, beliefs, such as his Hidden Associations (which include suppressed memories) and his Holy Grail, become part of a human's identity. In theory, humans invest a lot of thought regarding their deepest beliefs and values. As a consequence, if you challenge a human's Holy Grail, he will likely believe you are questioning his intelligence, which can mean trouble for you.

Changing a human's opinion regarding minor issues is usually okay.

Trying to change his super-self, however, is a far greater challenge. It takes lots of time and often a shocking event, like the loss of a job, a traumatic relationship break-up or the death of a family member. Yes, humans are more malleable under overwhelming stress. However, even then, it is difficult to change a human's vanity because, in the end, he must change it himself.

So, as a rule, we usually ignore this option; it requires too much work and time, and positive results are not always achievable. It's usually best to play with the cards dealt — the current super-self.

CONCLUSIONS

So, humans' vanity is central in their lives, and it begins to form based on what they admire or are proud of. Pay attention to these things and your prey will become more predictable. You will know, better than him, what guides his decisions.

The Holy Grail is a GOAL, but the primary influence it has on a human is the DIRECTION it leads him to take; it defines his vanity. Knowing a human's Holy Grail will enable you to always be a few steps ahead.

What makes a human feel pleasant or unpleasant sensations? It's simple: When closer to his Holy Grail he feels good; farther away, he feels bad. And events outside a human's Line of Power usually have little impact on his emotions. An easy concept most humans misunderstand.

The tricky part is you must have a clear image of your prey's Holy Grail.

Finally, it is worth repeating that it is true that the concept of a Holy Grail, or super-self, is a simplification of several ideas. However, applying it provides you, the hunter, with an edge. You can manipulate your prey by knowing, better than it does, where it's going and what will arouse its desire.

In the next chapter we provide tips for identifying your prey's Holy Grail. You'll learn that some humans have pre-packaged solutions, and why some humans are extra vulnerable. You'll find it quite interesting, we're sure.

11
VANITY
PRACTICAL TIPS

So, applying the Holy Grail concept makes it easy to predict a human's next steps. However, first, we must again warn you: It is not easy to identify a human's mission.

To understand a human's Holy Grail, or super-self, you must pay him close attention for some time. You will need several small clues that, put together, can provide a bigger picture. As usual, be careful not to jump to conclusions; you do need a minimum amount of evidence. For example, if a human owns some luxury items, that doesn't necessarily mean he cares only for money and social acceptance. It could, in fact, mean many other things.

By being hasty, you can fall into the same trap that many humans find themselves ensnared in when their Hidden Associations use small clues to reach premature conclusions. To become a great hunter takes patience.

A few helpful questions are:
- *"What is the meaning of success for this creature?"*
- *"What is it proud of?"*
- *"What is its super-self like?"*

Now, to make hunting easier, we highlight some common quests that humans pursue.

COMMON TYPES OF HOLY GRAILS

<u>Pre-packaged and fixed solutions</u>
In general, humans consider their super-selves to be linked to intelligence, beauty, money, family and a particular sexuality — like a smart, rich, handsome, heterosexual human with a beautiful partner and kids.

Humans most often struggle to understand that there are several other ways to be successful and they give little thought to the idea. They simply follow pre-packaged super-selves that their social group dictates, and they are often unwilling to change. *"There is only one solution, and I must pursue it!"*

When the only possible super-self is to be intelligent, rich, beautiful and with successful kids — when there is just one fixed mission — humans often end up slipping into denial to cope with reality.

For example, a father asks a close friend to train his son to be an executive, which follows the father's idea of a super-self. A few weeks later, the friend tells the father, sincerely trying to help, that his son can't process data (his son is dumb in this area, can't deal with numbers and business is not at all his thing). So, the friend recommends that the youngster pursues an alternative career that better suits his abilities because he is very good at sport, music, art and dealing with people.

What does the father do? Well, to him, being an executive is the route to becoming wealthy — his super-self. And, he believes this is the only possible path for his son. Also, the father's super-self wants a successful child. Consequently, he projects the same definition of success onto his son.

Because of his limited view, the father will probably see his friend as an enemy — an obstacle in the way of his Holy Grail — and become angry. He will refuse to listen to his 'enemy' and deny that there is a problem because he can't see any other route to success. Accepting that the kid isn't very smart is too painful and threatening (remember the extremes of the Drawers?). Like the captain and crew, for the father there is but one 'safe island', and his son will get there. As a result, instead of recognising the limitations and adapting, because that is too much to swallow, he denies the truth and distorts reality to cope.

So, for humans like the father described with a pre-packaged and fixed definition of success for himself and his children, any obstacle can be an extremely 'bitter pill to swallow'. They use denial and blame to cope with reality. As explained when we discussed the concept of Repetition, it's no wonder that humans continue to face the same problems all their lives.

<u>Other pre-packaged solutions</u>
Religions and beliefs, like left- and right-wing extremism in politics, also strongly influence the goals humans strive for. You see, religion provides a rigid set of moral codes and rules to follow — a template for a human's super-self. Easy, no? All done. No major reflection needed.

By the way, often religion also offers humans increased social acceptance and can help them feel part of a group, which feels good. Oh, and of course, there is also the 'get-into-heaven-and-stay-out-of-hell card'. So, all in all, religion provides a complete package for humans to build their vanity upon.

<u>Note:</u> Funnily enough, if you repeat what we say about religion to other humans, bearing in mind their broken communication system, they will probably think that we oppose their beliefs, that we deny there is life after death, which isn't true. We are just listing the benefits.

Extreme politics, both left and right, also offers most of what religion promises (except heaven after life is substituted for heaven on Earth once the enemy is crushed). And extremism allows humans to blame others for their problems. It provides convenient enemies. As we saw with the Weak Captain, blame is a useful 'anaesthetic' for numbing the pain of life's real problems.

For humans, in a world flooded with too much freedom of choice, pre-packaged sets of rules and objects of blame — even heaven — provide much relief.

Actually, for humans, pre-packaged solutions are a damned good deal because coming up with definitions of success by themselves is usually quite tricky — especially as their definitions may clash with those of close friends and family. So, it's best to ignore free thinking and follow the well-trodden path. Or, at least that seems to be the rationale. After all, any human who wishes to develop original ideas would soon discover that doing so takes lots of time and reflection. As is their nature, humans usually take the path of least resistance.

So, keep these standard packages in mind because you can get pretty reliable tips regarding what your prey's Holy Grail is by observing its surroundings, location (region on the planet), culture and religion, etc. Yes, you still should analyse your human prey separately and patiently, but remember that he has most likely thought little about his mission and is merely following the herd. Easy.

SUPER-VULNERABLE HUMANS

It's worth mentioning a few more vulnerable states of mind. If any of these relate to your prey, consider yourself lucky. Your hunt will be extra easy.

<u>Very narrow and specific missions</u>
For a human, a significant problem arises when his Holy Grail is based on one thing, and it doesn't depend on him. For example, *"Success is money,"* or *"Success is marriage."* When a goal is extra specific and depends on others, things become interesting, to say the least.

Having a single, specific definition of success is extremely risky for humans; a small 'bump in the road' can pose a considerable threat and be devastating.

On the other hand, a more balanced, self-reliant definition leaves the prey less vulnerable. For example, success could mean a combination of having a great family, a certain amount of money and work-life balance. When there is a threat to one of these things, the human's mission isn't entirely at risk (we will deal with exceptions later).

It's simple: If your prey has a balanced super-self, it's difficult to pose significant threats.

So, whenever you can, avoid these balanced humans. As a rule, those with poorly crafted missions (a pure *"I want to be rich,"* or *"I want to be a great husband or wife"*) are usually easier to catch.

Conflict within the mission (two Holy Grails)

Humans with two conflicting missions, with no chance of achieving either, and no room for negotiation, are usually extra vulnerable and, like 'fish in a barrel', easy to skewer. They're like a ship with two opposing missions that it must pursue simultaneously.

It's like a married male human who wants a peaceful life and abide by all the requirements of his religion (which requires monogamy in his marriage). However, at the same time, he is proud of having many affairs with multiple females. For him, manhood is measured by the number of females he can seduce. So, to get closer to one of his super-selves, he must do things that conflict with the other(s).

Or, in another example, a human who strives to become a business leader in a highly competitive market, which most probably means he must work excessively long hours for decades. At the same time, however, he wishes to spend plenty of time with his kids and be what is known as a "family guy". This human can't see a way of getting closer to his first goal without drifting farther away from his second.

Finally, imagine a human who wants to be a successful executive to please his father, but to make himself and his mother happy, he wants to be an artist. The human will be in constant conflict unless he stops and defines his mission, or finds some way to achieve both Holy Grails.

As another general rule, humans without well-defined missions are usually more susceptible to manipulation due to the problems that conflicting Holy Grails bring to their lives. Pay attention to these humans.

Full-package humans (multiple Holy Grails)

Some humans have a super-self that includes most of the points mentioned above and more.

For example, a human may want to be the best son, husband and father; a powerful executive with work-life balance; he may strive to meet his religious requirements; on top of all this, he may fancy himself as the local *Don Juan* who beds multiple females.

So, this full-package human continually contradicts his Line of Power. Whenever he gets close to one goal and feels good, he drifts farther away from several others and feels bad.

A human like this hardly ever reaches a reasonable level of

satisfaction, and he is easy to seduce and manipulate if you convince him that you can help with his struggle.

Full-package humans usually crave social acceptance from everyone, which results in a need to be what everyone wants them to be. As simple as that. They lack reflection and have an extreme need for acceptance due to insecurity.

FULL-PACKAGE HUMANS

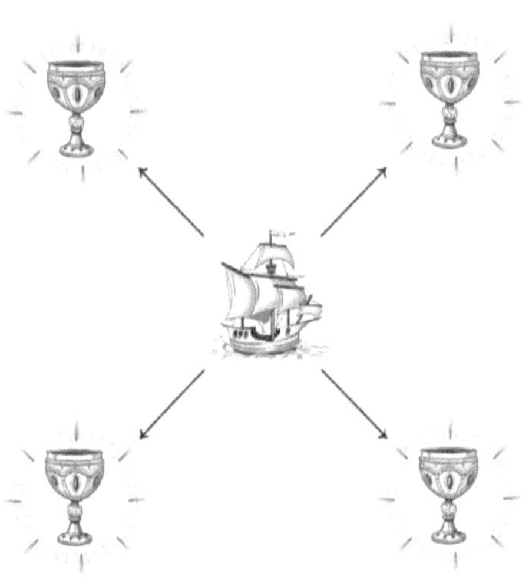

Figure 2. Full-package humans

***

<u>Tip:</u> Start with an easy prey, one with a specific, fixed and narrow mission. This kind of human usually has a low understanding of the complexities of life. Or, pick one with conflicting missions who won't accept compromise (even better if it is a full-package human). This kind is usually especially vulnerable and easy to manipulate and hunt.

***

CONCLUSIONS

So, surroundings, location (region on the planet), culture and religion can provide excellent tips for identifying your prey's Holy Grail. Pay attention to all these things.

Although humans often follow pre-packaged solutions, keep in mind that the super-self a human pursues can be very different from other humans, so never jump to conclusions based on minimal evidence.

Also, remember that some humans are extra vulnerable due to poorly crafted missions. Consider yourself a lucky hunter if you stumble upon one of them.

In the next chapter, you will see how a humans' self-interest is crucial in their lives and how the concept of a Holy Grail is vital for understanding our expanded version of self-interest. It is an important chapter because, whether intimidating or enthralling your prey, you must always appeal to its self-interest — the lever that drives humans. It might be obvious for you, but we must ensure that you have this concept crystal clear in your mind before we explore toying with humans' fears.

12

SCEPTICAL TO THE BONE
SELF-INTEREST EXPANDED

"Something may be better for humanity, the planet, the country, the city, the company — even my family — but how is it better for me?"

Though they wouldn't admit it, this is the question every human asks before taking action — even if oblivious to the fact.

Again, what we are about to point out, at first glance, will seem like something of a cosmetic change, even too sceptical. However, thinking *"What's in it for my prey?"* is a crucial shift in how you should view things from now on. You see, knowing the benefit your prey will receive by acting a certain way is the final piece of the puzzle you need before you can toy with its fears.

As a hunter, you must study the world through the lens of self-interest. Then, and only then, will you understand human beings and their behaviours.

While hunting, keep this in mind at all times: Every second of the day that humans work, play, relax, sleep, or do anything else, they are doing what they believe is best for them — from helping an old lady cross the street to tearing wings off flies.

A human's actions ALWAYS, ALWAYS, again, ALWAYS start

with self-interest, which is the lever that drives them. Failing to understand this fact is being blind to reality — like living in a fairy tale.

Of course, some actions are more useful — desirable — to society than others. What matters to us, though, is that every single human focuses on what they believe is the best for them. Though all concepts in this book are important, to better understand the levers of self-interest, the Holy-Grail concept should be particularly helpful.

First, though, we must clarify what we are NOT saying when we discuss the concept of self-interest.

CLARIFICATION:
CYNICISM ON EARTH

Consider our explanation about self-interest carefully. Don't jump to premature conclusions. As the authors of this book, if we're not careful, we risk resembling those cynical humans who claim the world is based on self-interest. And we don't want that.

You see, while on Earth, you will hear some humans saying things like, *"Everybody is selfish; greed drives the world." "I see the world as it is. You are too naïve — I can see it better than you."* And you may think these statements are similar to what we are saying in this chapter. However, this is not the case.

If you dig deep, you'll discover that statements like *"Everybody is selfish, and greed drives the world"* reek with resentment and come from the lips of animals with limited understanding of themselves. The rationale seems to be *"Don't expect anything and you will not be disappointed,"* or, even better, *"Expect the worst from everyone."*

Tear the mask off these thoroughly 'sceptical warriors', and you will look upon the face of a frightened animal that spurns hope to avoid disappointment. This mindset is a defence mechanism for the weak — a shelter for wounded animals unable to cope with disappointment. There is more to it than that, though: These animals feed off their sceptical self-image to feel like they are smarter than others.

Of course, this is not the case with us.

So, let's be clear: For humans, cynicism is usually a defence, not an objective and more realistic view of human nature. For you to understand how warped the perspective of these sceptical humans is, their version of self-interest only considers the rewards of money, recognition and acceptance, and ignores the role emotions play. Consequently, humans fail to understand self-interest and the entire spectrum of human nature from the get-go.

We are NOT talking about the same things. We are merely sceptical and focused hunters attempting to explain the rationale and weakness of these humans. We concentrate on what goes on within the mind of our prey and take advantage. And, of course, like any animal with minimal brain capacity, with humans, self-interest — or at least our version of it — is a key driver.

So, yes, we say that, at all times, self-interest is the lever that drives all animals — humans are no exception. As you read this chapter, you will understand that our concept is far broader than that of sceptical, cynical humans.

OUR VERSION OF SELF-INTEREST

To understand humans' Expanded Self-Interest, first you must delve deep into their minds because, fundamentally, all humans seek the same thing. The difference, though, is that they have wildly different ways of achieving it — as you saw in the nonsensical Hidden Associations that humans create that link to often unrelated things and cause absurd behaviours.

Here's an extreme example:

<u>Tell a human this story: Altruist/selfless rescuer</u>
On the way to a long-awaited, potentially life-changing job interview, a human notices a child drowning in a river. There are other young children screaming for help; none, though, are capable of helping the drowning boy. There is no time to make an emergency phone call, and the human knows that getting involved will be dangerous, as well as result in him missing his interview — there will be no other opportunity to win his dream job. So, he hesitates. For this human, however, there is no alternative, and he dives into the river.

<u>How does this apply to humans? And how can you use it against them?</u>
Before we answer, ask yourself this: Did the human perform a heroic act WITHOUT seeking anything in return?

Before concluding what actually happened, we must explain our concept of self-interest further by taking an alternative approach. We will return to this example later in the chapter.

Our concept of self-interest

Three major things influence how the human brain behaves:

1.   Human rewards EXPANDED.
2.   Its desire to maximise good things and minimise the bad.
3.   Its capacity to consider the long-term.

<u>1. Human rewards expanded</u>

Humans generally have a limited view of their rewards system. Many can see only one: money (or any kind of resource), or, at most, money, recognition and acceptance. So, humans tend to think that whenever another acts without expecting one of these rewards, that they are doing so for nothing in return. As we said, this is a mistake — human beings are way more complicated than that.

To summarise the many and crazy ways the brain rewards beyond money, recognition and acceptance, the Holy Grail concept helps considerably. Yes, a human's pursuit of his super-self plays a significant role; after all, when nearing his Holy Grail, his brain rewards him — he feels good.

Yes! This chapter also requires a good understanding of *The Brain's Puppet* chapter; after all, when explaining our expanded version of self-interest, human emotions and desires play a pivotal role.

So, given humans' ignorance, if you expand your understanding of rewards beyond the three that are obvious, your mindset will be starkly different to most humans.

<u>2. Maximising good things and minimising the bad. Simple. Or, it should be.</u>

It is crucial for you to understand this: All humans seek to maximise pleasure and minimise pain and suffering, which, by the way, seems so simple that it is weird that we have to explain. However, you wouldn't believe how many humans question this rationale.

Yes, our concept is simple. However, it requires closer inspection because some cases look strange — like when a human enjoys pain or sacrifice because he believes he is getting closer to heaven. The assumptions humans make to reach their Holy Grail vary widely.

But, it's not only Holy Grails or Hidden Associations that are to blame, and this is why humans don't fully understand our concept of seeking pleasure and avoiding pain. A human's capacity to see the long-term consequences of his actions also affects many of his decisions.

3. The long-term view: *"Can my prey see the long-term?"*

Just like it would be impossible to get a dog to have a vaccine by trying to convince it of the long-term benefits, some humans can't understand or see benefits beyond a few years, weeks — or even minutes.

You see, most believe our concept of maximising pleasure and minimising pain relates to short-term — immediate — rewards. This is a misinterpretation of the rule we use — for dogs that can't see beyond the next 'belly-rub'. No, our concept is much bigger, and humans whose actions lead to pain or discomfort strive towards long-term rewards: pain eventually leading to heaven, or study leading to success, for example.

So, you will see that the decisions some humans make focus on bad things first — pain, instead of pleasure — and you, therefore, may think we are talking rubbish. Seeing humans toiling at awful jobs, sacrificing holidays for others, etc., may make you question the rule of maximising good stuff and minimising the bad. Dig deeply enough, though, and you will discover that the human will always hold assumptions that his choices are better for him in the short- or long-term.

The rewards humans seek are not always plain to see, as they can come in many forms: social recognition, feelings of satisfaction or, perhaps, a promised magical afterlife, for example.

You see, despite being obvious, humans struggle to accept that they want to maximise pleasure and minimise pain.

So, they refute the idea because:

- They don't understand the complexity of the Hidden Associations in the human mind.
- They think it is just an immediate pleasure or pain analysis when, in fact, it is a far more complicated process of considering the long-term effects of decisions.

Anyway, that's their problem.

For us, *"Can my prey see the long-term?"* is a question you should always ask because the answer will affect your tactics. After all, teasing your quarry with a long-term reward if it can only see the short-term is pointless, right?

So, it's worth pointing out that not all humans have the same capacity when it comes to processing data; the ability to analyse and interpret situations varies considerably among humans. Consequently, differing abilities will affect how humans analyse situations and reach conclusions.

To understand your prey, you should, therefore, not only understand its assumptions and the many rewards its brain applies, but you should also determine whether or not it can see the long-term.

<u>Why can't some humans see the long-term?</u>

Here are some easy-to-remember reasons why some humans can't see the long-term:

- They have a low capacity to process data (they're dumb).
- They are poorly educated and haven't been taught to consider future consequences.
- They were spoiled as children.

So, the first reason is a problem with the individual, the second with the education system (or lack of access to it) and with the third, although also related to education, a problem with the individual's parents or caregivers.

The reason *They were spoiled as children* is interesting because of its similarity to the second; however, it is worth highlighting separately because it affects some highly educated humans and can cause misunderstandings.

Yes, spoiled humans also don't develop the capacity to analyse pleasure returns in the long-term. Humans are not born with the capacity to analyse long-term pleasure returns. It's a learned ability that those who were spoiled during childhood, and forever satisfied in the short-term, never needed to develop. Their parents screwed them. As simple as that.

It's also worth highlighting that your prey's ability to think long-term is influenced by the situation or environment that it finds itself in.

It's like a starving human, although highly intelligent, he can't think too much about the future. He needs food now!

So, always double-check your prey's long-term capacity when selecting the bait to use.

Interestingly, in a next chapter, you will see how some humans (even the wealthy) spend their whole lives behaving like desperate, cornered and starving animals that continually fight for survival (even when they seem safe and satisfied). You will learn how to identify these 'fat dogs', that are desperate for the next steak and use their behaviour against them. Wait and see!

Now, before we explain self-interest and the consequences further, let's look at some real-life situations.

HUMAN SELF-INTEREST APPLIED

We will begin this section by describing something humans understand better than themselves: business.

<u>Tell a human this story: A sustainable company</u>

A company changes its portfolio to sustainable products — those that are good for the planet. It also establishes a foundation to help the environment, etc., etc.

A good proportion of humans will guess that, behind this new behaviour, there are assumptions and strategies.

For example, the company may assume that customers will pay more for sustainable products, and a move to sustainability will strengthen its brand and equity. The company may also believe that it will sell more products with less marketing expenditure and increase profits, even though its new products are more expensive to manufacture.

Maybe the company sees being sustainable as a trend that it must comply with to survive.

Or, perhaps it figures being sustainable is an inexpensive way to attract fresh talent.

The company might also conclude that it is so big that, without change, its negative impact will be so severe that there will be a backlash in the future.

Maybe it's not a company, a not-for-profit instead, and the owner wants to feel good (get closer to his Holy Grail) by doing something beneficial for the planet.

Of course, these are just a few of many possible assumptions. Whatever the strategy is, the world is still a jungle, especially for businesses. So, unless there is some 'squillionaire' willing to spend a fortune to compensate for bad stuff he has done, or a dreamer who can't analyse the long-term outcomes of his actions, there will be an assumption behind the company's strategy that its move is better for the company. And, most (or at least smart) humans understand this.

<u>How does this apply to humans? And how can you use it against them?</u>
There is always a trade-off. Like the company, humans also have assumptions. The difference, though, is that they are often unaware of them — they translate assumptions and conclusions into EMOTIONS and DESIRES. But, make no mistake, the Messenger (the brain) processes everything in the background, and humans' ignorance towards their self-interest won't change this.

Using the rationale of the example above, when a father helps his daughter, he may claim to expect nothing in return. And, he will be telling the truth regarding visible rewards, like money or recognition.

However, humans struggle to grasp that the father enjoys seeing his child happy and thinking of himself as a good parent, etc. Whatever it is, there is always an expected return for anything a human does.

Let's take a more complex and sceptical view of things to help you understand humans and their flaws.

THE SCEPTICAL BRAIN

So, make no mistake: When a human goes to sleep, to a job he hates, or has fun, he is always doing what he believes is best for him given the options he has or can see. From the brain's perspective, there is no such a thing as a random action — or one without an expected reward, if you consider the expanded version of a brain's rewards.

Rewards can come in the form of desires, emotions, feelings, sensations — all that stuff. It's true that humans are not always cognisant of all the assumptions and conclusions their brains make in the background, but that doesn't change the fact that assumptions and conclusions are there. If you think that your prey did something randomly, you are, without a doubt, wrong. You are missing a piece of the puzzle. You somehow failed to understand its brain's assumptions that led to the action.

<u>Slaves too</u>

Here's another extreme case: A slave follows his master's orders because doing so is best for him. It's a terrible option, but, still, he chooses to obey. *"Let's see. Should I receive a jolly good thrashing or work hard?"*

<u>How about suicide?</u>

Even a human who commits suicide falls within this rationale. As we've said, all of Earth's creatures seek to maximise good stuff and minimise the bad based on choices they have or can see. It doesn't make sense to do anything else.

So, if a human kills himself, we could suppose that he was so desperately miserable that he thought the best option to minimise the shit in his life was death. He probably chose suicide because, given his life seemed unbearable, according to his inner analysis, he thought suicide was the best possible option. So, the rationale is the same, even if it means having nothing. Zero is better than a negative number. Suicide is a fundamental failure of hope but still falls within the rationale of maximising the good stuff and minimising bad.

In a less extreme example, which is the primary focus of this explanation, your human prey's choice of career, lover, or simply whether to rest or not, is the product of desires his brain transmits based on what it thinks is best for him.

<u>Even a gift of flowers?</u>

Let's look at a human who gives flowers to his partner. He may make this romantic gesture to feel like he is kind or because he likes to see her smile. Maybe he enjoys seeing his partner happy because then she'll be nicer to him. Maybe he likes to see himself as a kind person. Whatever the reason, giving flowers is for his benefit first.

The same rationale applies to every human — from filthy politicians to the finest humans on Earth.

<u>The shifting paradigm that changes everything:</u>
Again, this may seem like a simple change in mindset — and somewhat sceptical — but understanding that humans always do what's right for them will help you to predict their behaviour considerably. When understanding a human's self-interest, it is possible to understand his society better.

A company, for example, does what's best for it, as well as the CEO, directors and employees. All parties have different financial situations, families, beliefs and Holy Grails. Sometimes their goals align, but other times they don't. Consequently:

- Something can be good for the planet and the company but not so great for the CEO and his next end-of-the-year bonus.
- Likewise, something can be good for the city but not for a citizen living on the street where construction will take place. How will the citizen vote?
- Moving to a new city can be good for a family but not for one family member.

So, when setting your bait and trap, consider carefully the interests of all humans involved in a situation.

Of course, a CEO or citizen on that street can do the 'right thing' in a situation, too. However, each will do so out of either fear of getting caught doing wrong, the pleasure of doing good, or because they have a Holy Grail that is related to being a good citizen, etc.

Remember, all humans are still animals. If a wealthy doctor complies with the law and doesn't steal a pack of beer from a supermarket, it is due to, all things considered, the risk of being caught, the affordability of beer for him, the rewards he already enjoys from being part of organised society, and the person he aspires to be. By paying for the beer, he receives the maximum reward.

So, the doctor prefers to pay for the beer because doing so is better for him. On the other hand, a human who steals the beer either finds it too expensive to pay for, or believes the consequences of getting caught are less worrying than the benefits of stealing. Of course, he could be proud of taking a risk, of doing the wrong thing. His Holy Grail can play a role here.

Yes, obeying the law or respecting human rights are choices humans make based on the rewards of living in a better society, or analysis of the consequences they may face if they don't. It's as simple as that (okay, maybe it is not so simple, but the rationale is).

In fact, from a strictly sceptical point of view, the number of years in prison, depending on the crime, works like a price list. A human might think, *"Can I rob a store? Sure, but if I get caught it can cost up to five years in prison. That's the price."* Then, he considers the trade-off by analysing the cost-risk-reward and makes a decision.

***

Applying this strictly sceptical rationale is crucial because it takes hope out of the equation when manipulating your prey. Any human will always do what is best for him. So, asking "How can I make the actions I want my prey to take look best for him?" is the way to go.

***

CLARIFICATION 2:
EXPANDED SELF-INTEREST IS NOT THE SAME AS SELFISHNESS

It's important to note that the so-called selfish human, or egoist, is merely a creature who derives (or can see) little to NO reward from anything that won't impact himself (directly).

As explained, every human seeks to increase the good stuff and decrease the bad, and the egoist is a human who is incapable of finding pleasure in good stuff if he isn't the beneficiary.

So, a selfish human can arise from a lack of capacity to see how doing kind deeds for others will benefit him now (i.e. make him feel better) or in the future. If he could see a benefit, maybe he would change and become a non-selfish animal. Simple.

BACK TO THE FIRST EXAMPLE

After all we have said in this chapter, you have probably figured out why the human chose to forgo his long-awaited job interview to save the drowning child.

If you recall, upon seeing the young boy in the water, he hesitated for a few seconds. However, for him, there was no alternative, so he dove into the water to save the drowning boy. What happened? Did the human act without expecting a reward?

By now, it should be clear that, in a case like this, humans will usually judge the rescuer's actions as selfless because they don't understand the types of rewards humans can seek.

Now, with the benefit of having almost completed this chapter, how far away do you think the 'heroic' rescuer would be from his Holy Grail if he'd let the boy drown? Given this human's Holy Grail, the super-self in his mind, there was almost no alternative — he had to help the boy.

You see, the trade-off was this: risk his interview (career, which links to more resources) compared to distancing himself from his Holy Grail forever (letting the boy die would be a crushing blow to his mission). He would be haunted by remorse and guilt for the rest of his life.

Of course, saving the boy should be considered a great act — well suited for human society — but it wasn't selfless; instead, the human wanted to get closer to his Holy Grail (or couldn't afford to slip away from it). He chose to help because he believed he would be better off to do so. The return for saving the boy would be far higher than the alternative.

CONCLUSIONS

The belief that some humans act for no reward is an extraordinarily compelling fantasy but one that we hunters cannot afford to entertain.

Keep in mind that your prey will always ask himself *"What is in it for me?"* So, to manipulate a human during a hunt, constantly put yourself in his shoes.

The self-interest mindset will help you understand human behaviour. Humans can seek rewards other than money, recognition and acceptance — their brain rewards in complex ways.

Remember, at least from the brain's perspective, there is no such thing as an act for no reward.

Like a dog trainer, the human brain reinforces and punishes, but in more complex ways. The paths to pleasure and suffering can vary widely depending on many factors, as we have discussed. After all, the human rewards system is complicated, but all brains follow the same principle of maximising the good stuff and minimising the bad.

Also, when hunting, consider whether or not the human is capable of processing data in order to see the long-term rewards.

If you understand your prey well (always using self-interest as a starting point), even when using minimal external stimuli, you will be able to manipulate it as you please.

In the next chapter, you will learn how to play with a human's fear. Yes, it is true that it is fun to enthral your prey by playing with its vanity and Holy Grail. However, if you must choose between playing with fear or vanity, remember the following words from a famous human:

***

"It is better to be feared than loved, if you cannot be both."
Niccolo Machiavelli

13
SURVIVAL MODE
FEAR

Now we are ready to delve into the most fun and effective approach for manipulating humans — playing with their fear. To understand how to do this, you must appreciate fear itself, how it works, and why humans most often live in fear that they artificially create.

Then, you will see how to manipulate your prey, depending on what it is afraid of.

Later, we will show you some common signs that identify a prey permanently haunted by fear.

As usual, it will sound a bit confusing at first, but you will get what we mean within a few pages.

FEAR & ITS CAUSES

<u>The animal detecting it is vulnerable</u>

As you have seen, the brain plays with a human's emotions to drive him towards the direction it wants. One of the most potent emotions at the brain's disposal is fear.

Fear, is more than an emotion, though. It is an unpleasant and overpowering feeling caused by a threat (or anticipation) of danger, pain

125

or harm. Fear is difficult to ignore. Play with fear, and you tap into the power of mother nature herself.

Fear has a critical survival-related function, and when triggered, it activates a range of defensive behaviours. When in jeopardy, animals often have little time to think, so they react using basic survival instincts and by producing a variety of fear-related responses. Frightened animals usually become more aggressive, reactive and alert. Their focus is often on attack or escape.

With non-human animals, fear is usually easy to recognise because the causes are plain to see and the creatures' reactions predictable. With these animals, external sources of danger, such as those associated with loud noises, threatening gestures and the proximity of other strange animals, are often the cause. Obvious stuff. These animals feel VULNERABLE, and their brains send signals of FEAR that then trigger a 'fight-or-flight' response. Frightened animals are in a state of alert that we call "Survival Mode".

For humans, as usual, things are more complicated, but the rationale is the same. And what is crucial is that, when scared, humans, like animals, are usually incapable of clear thought, and they merely react. So, humans, too, feel vulnerable and switch to Survival Mode. That's the state you want your prey to be in during a hunt because it is likely to make desperate moves, stupid mistakes and will be prone to manipulation.

Vulnerability isn't only linked to fear

So, it is true that for any animal — including a human being — fear is a reaction caused by its brain detecting that its body might be vulnerable, so the animal enters Survival Mode.

However, this feeling of vulnerability can take many forms, and some can be misleading: examples are anger, nervousness, extreme hate, frequent anxiety, high levels of stress, or sometimes even aggression. An animal can feel any of these emotions when its brain believes its body is vulnerable. The animal is reacting to a perceived threat that it is unsure it can handle. It's the unbearable feeling of lacking the power to deal with the possible danger that causes the problem.

Interestingly, among humans, anger and aggression are often confused with signs of power, instead of weakness related to vulnerability. And in case we haven't yet convinced you that they are signs of vulnerability, we will have by the time you finish this chapter.

Survival Mode is (or was) useful

Survival Mode is what drives most animals most of the time. But don't get us wrong. In the savannah, fear is what keeps animals alert and alive. After all, at any time in the wild, a tiger or a venomous snake can strike. So, of course, fear, which heightens an animal's alertness, is vital in dangerous situations. Any creature will switch to a state of anxiety from time to time due to the nature of life on Earth. Remember, many survive by eating each other. What else can you expect?

It was no different for humans; living in constant alertness and fear was once essential for survival. Until recently, humans needed weapons (rocks, swords, guns, etc.) to avoid death or subjugation. In modern times, though, a new reality has dawned — or at least for most humans.

Luckily, as you will see, almost all humans still spend their lives in in a state of alert — even though they are not wholly aware of the fact. Yes, based on our experience, the vast majority live almost their entire lives in Survival Mode — scared like cornered and starving animals, even when they are perfectly safe, and food is abundant.

As weird as it sounds, the vast majority of humans still live in some auto-generated (almost) permanent state of alert. Fear in humans is often overused, which creates serious problems for them: poor reasoning and desperate reactions that increase mistakes and vulnerability to attack, for example.

So, Survival Mode was once useful for humans. Now, though, it is helpful mainly for us because it reduces their rationality to similar levels of Earth's other less challenging animals.

How can we state that humans are (almost) permanently in Survival Mode?

Simply put, if you consider other emotions, such as nervousness and stress (losing one's temper in general), as signs of an animal in Survival Mode, and if you observe humans for even a short time, you can quickly conclude that most of them, most of the time, are either in or on the verge of being there. The rationale is simple: A human who becomes nervous or stressed easily can (also easily) feel vulnerable, so he needs to be permanently alert.

<u>Imaginary needs: A major source of the problem.</u>
Survival Mode always starts with dissatisfaction. There is, without fail, something lacking. So a human FEELS he NEEDS something essential and, therefore, believes he is being deprived.

The trick is that humans almost always think they NEED more than they do. They are unaware that we can only attack or threaten to take away something they need, not what they want. Well, at least, attacking a want is not nearly as effective.

As you will see, humans most often feel that they lack something essential, and so they pursue whatever it is desperately — even when they don't need it — like a fat dog bounding huffing and puffing in pursuit of a juicy steak.

Believe it or not, humans tend to suffer more from imagination than reality by creating unnecessarily high needs for survival and being afraid of not meeting them, and this fact creates a tremendous opportunity for hunters. Consequently, you can easily manipulate humans' fears and create an artificial Survival Mode within their minds. These hapless creatures already do the same thing themselves. Imagine how easy it would be for you to create manufactured — imaginary — fears.

But, what is this something that humans believe that they lack and need?

THE MINIMUM REQUIREMENTS — AN OVERVIEW

Let's look at a simple example.

<u>Tell a human this story: The minimum requirements for the captain to control his ship.</u>
Imagine the same captain on the ancient ship — yes, we are going to use him again. The ship also seeks a Holy Grail, the perfect island, but before pursuing it, the captain needs to take control of his ship.

*For the captain to have full control of his vessel, his crew must feel minimally safe. For this to happen, there must be a minimum amount of **resources** (food, guns, gold, the ship is in a seaworthy* *condition, etc.),* **alliances** *with other vessels, and a certain level of* **trust in the captain***.*

Without these things, the ship enters, what we call, "Survival Mode", and it is tough for the captain to lead the crew. **Resources, alliances and trust in the captain***: These are the requirements for the crew to feel SAFE and to FOLLOW the captain's orders. Without them, the captain CANNOT fully CONTROL his ship.*

Interestingly, not all ships require the same level of resources and alliances to function well.

You see, whether or not the crew feels safe depends a lot on how much they trust the captain's capabilities. If they perceive him as a weak leader, they will only feel safe with many resources (a fantastic ship, extra food, a massive arsenal of guns and endless pieces of gold) and alliances that could lend a hand when in trouble. Conversely, a great leader may still lead a calm crew even in a worst-case scenario (like a terrible storm or an attack from another ship) with far fewer resources or alliances, although, of course, they still need some.

<u>How does this apply to humans? And how can you use it against them?</u>
Humans follow the same rationale as the ship described. They are just more complicated, as you will see; when humans fall below a minimum level of Resources, Alliances or Trust in the Captain, they switch to Survival Mode and can't fully control themselves — like the captain can't control his ship.

This concept may sound confusing, but the rationale is simple: Before pursuing his Holy Grail, a human must first focus on survival. He needs to feel his life isn't in peril. And for this to happen, a human must fulfil some minimum requirements.

And, when humans lack things, like the ship's crew, they feel vulnerable, which leads to fear, anxiety, anger — losing their temper and all that stuff related to Survival Mode — which, as you know, lowers their rationality and control.

To make things clear, check out the diagram below. We have added a line representing the minimum requirements to that shown in the chapter *Personal Holy Grail.*

HUMANS IN SURVIVAL MODE
Below the minimal level of requirements

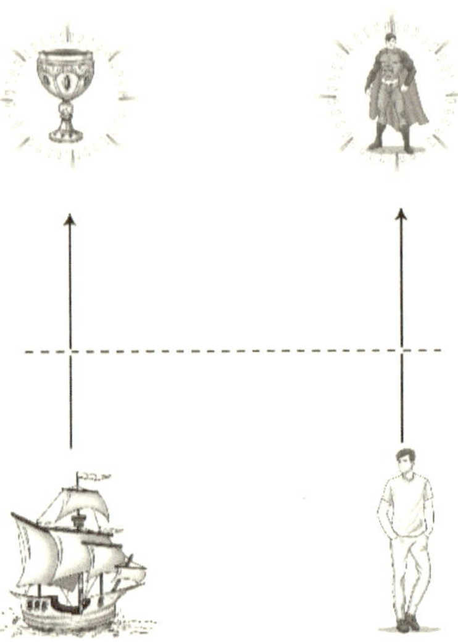

Figure 3. The minimal level of requirements.

Naturally, when below the minimal level of requirements, the brain alerts an animal that its life is in peril. Once these minimum requirements are fulfilled, though, the animal is freer to pursue its Holy Grail.

So, the main differences between the two situations are as follows:

- When a creature is above the line, he chases what he WANTS — his vanity, etc. Problems on the way usually cause some discomfort or disappointment, but nothing major.
- On the other hand, when in Survival Mode, where a creature is in desperate pursuit of what it believes it NEEDS to survive, even minor problems lead it to lose its temper and become aggressive. Anything can look threatening.

Also, just like ships with strong or weak captains, not all humans have the same minimum requirements for Resources and Alliances to feel safe. Some need only a few; others require the whole universe! So, depending on your prey, this line can be high or low. And, like on the ship, minimum requirements depend on the level of Trust in the Captain each human has.

The three requirements
If an animal meets its minimum requirements of basics such as air, food, water and shelter, it has enough to live and hunt alone. If, however, the animal is a social beast, like a hyena, wolf or chimpanzee (that depends on a group for hunting and survival), it will also need a minimum level of group acceptance.

So, given that humans are social, they have similar requirements to that of hyenas, wolves and chimpanzees. Humans need Resources AND Alliances.

Humans require a minimum amount of Resources (such as food, shelter, health and money), Alliances (such as acceptance of a group, love and connections) and, finally, Trust in the Captain (such as self-esteem and confidence).

What about sex? Is that a consideration, and how should you label it?

Well, for many animals, carnal relations are essential, indeed. For others, not so much. Some can even live without sex. So, the answer to the question of where sex comes into play is not straightforward. Culture, age, hormones and an animal's Holy Grail, etc., all influence its importance.

How to label sex? Well, you can assign it to Alliances (for obvious reasons) or Resources (if you consider sex could help, for example, with your prey's health). Anyway, you get the idea.

Future perspectives: There is one big difference between humans and other animals: Humans are more able to think in the long-term. The FUTURE influences them more. So, for Resources and Alliances, you shouldn't analyse just the present moment. After all, if a human has enough for today but is worried that he will lack Resources (i.e. money) in the future, he will still focus on gathering more Resources now.

So, a human can still be in Survival Mode because of a perceived future. Therefore, when determining your prey's need for Resources, consider his future perspectives (savings, a good job or access to money farther down the track, etc.) or whatever he needs to believe he is minimally safe. And the same applies if a human thinks he has the acceptance of a group now but is worried it may vanish tomorrow.

So, there are three factors that determine whether a human feels safe: Resources, Alliances and Trust in the Captain. And, it's these three cards that we will deal regarding fear. Pretty simple, right? Just remember to consider the present AND future perspectives, and you'll be fine.

But before we go any further, let us make one thing clear.

CLARIFICATION:
THE HIERARCHY OF NEEDS ON EARTH

While on Earth, you may hear of a concept called the "Hierarchy of Needs" that seems similar to what we are about to explain.

Yes, the Hierarchy of Needs is a similar concept to ours. We combine and label needs differently, though, so that they are easier to remember, but it is roughly the same thing. Use whatever works.

Yes, indeed, many humans know of the Hierarchy of Needs concept. HOWEVER, they often fail to understand that those needs are an individual's PERCEPTIONS which are influenced by Hidden Associations and Drawers.

Without considering perceptions and Hidden Associations, the theory is USELESS. As usual, it may sound like we are just playing with semantics. However, understanding that needs are an individual's perceptions, which are influenced by Hidden Associations and Drawers, is the difference between applying the concept correctly or not.

THE INFLUENCE HIDDEN ASSOCIATIONS & DRAWERS
HAVE ON MINIMUM REQUIREMENTS

<u>PERCEIVED minimum requirements</u>

Humans struggle to understand that a millionaire can be in Survival Mode because he feels he lacks Resources (in this case money). They know that some humans want more, but most would struggle to believe a millionaire could feel vulnerable because he lacks money.

Indeed, it sounds odd and contradictory, but cases like this are typical. Yes, a wealthy human can be well below his basic needs for Resources — even with millions of dollars in his bank account.

PERCEIVED is the keyword in both our concept and that of the Hierarchy of Needs. And humans almost never know this fact. As a result, most fail to see that a millionaire can have bizarrely high minimum requirements for money and so be permanently in Survival Mode, even though he might seem entirely satisfied.

Yes, given that wealthy humans have so many Resources, it seems strange that they could fear losing some of them. However, let's review two possible reasons for such a situation:

- Hidden Associations: A wealthy human could link money with social approval or be compensating for insecurity, among many other things. So, deep inside, sometimes it is not Resources he lacks or frets about; it could be Alliances (social approval) — despite money being what he feels has sent him to Survival Mode. Indeed, humans are complicated animals.

- Few Drawers: If, for example, a wealthy human has only two categories in his mind, (winners and losers), the idea of losing a little money could send him spiralling to the Loser Drawer and directly to Survival Mode. Consequently, this human sways from well above his minimum requirements (where he feels safe) to far below — to the dangerous Survival Mode. It is a direct jump. A big fall. And worst of all is that even before a problem happens, this human dreads the fact that it (the big fall) is a possibility. There is so much at stake all the time.

So, these humans continually try to acquire more Resources, such as money, and Alliances, such as social acceptance and friends, and they are afraid of losing any of them.

Note: Interestingly, in the case of a human with only two Drawers, acquiring more money is useless. Given that he can see only extremes, no matter how far from Survival Mode the human is, he will plummet straight to it when he jumps from the Winner to Loser Drawer. And, yet, he keeps chasing more money. Haha!

And the same goes for all needs. Humans can have excessive minimum requirements for them all. The reason humans need so much to feel safe is that, just like in the case of the millionaire desperate for money, their needs are usually related to insecurity and substituted with other stuff. So, for example, a human is insecure and afraid of not being socially approved, so he needs thousands of friends to show him that he is okay. And he is scared of losing any of them. Weird.

Can you see how not knowing about Hidden Association or Drawers makes the Hierarchy of Needs theory useless for most humans?

One consequence of Hidden Associations — and even the Drawers — is the emergence of imaginary threats.

Real versus fake threats: starving versus Fat Dogs
Naturally, we expect an animal (human or otherwise) to be nervous when there is a REAL THREAT; that's the purpose of fear. As it should be, the Survival Mode is on.

By a *real* threat, we mean a significant problem: an animal under attack from a predator, or a human in desperate need of a job to buy food and pay the rent, for example. Real problems. We compare those in real need to a starving dog desperate for food. After all, it is, indeed, in Survival mode and really does need more Resources.

However, it's not that simple. The power of human imagination can create a flood of opportunities for us. As we said, for humans, there are both real and artificially created problems. We call those facing the latter "Fat Dogs".

Fat Dogs: Yes, some humans behave like belching, drooling, fat dogs. They already have enough food, but they hunger for more and whine if they miss the next steak. Fat Dogs desperately scramble towards wherever you throw the steak — unaware that they don't need it. And, this particular weakness is fun to explore. Just like a millionaire desperate for money, Fat Dogs artificially create high needs of which they are desperate to fulfil.

A straightforward example of this happening is when a human confuses his Holy Grail (super-self) with a NEED he MUST achieve. Instead of a guide, his Holy Grail becomes a requirement.

Whenever something becomes a minimum requirement for an animal to feel safe, things become interesting because the animal is desperate.

So, a consequence of Hidden Associations is the frequent occurrence of high minimum requirements for humans to feel safe, which causes fake threats. Look deeply, and you will discover that having a high minimum level of needs is a sign of insecurity and weakness.

HIGH MINIMUM-LEVEL REQUIREMENTS
A sign of weakness

<u>Tell a human this story: The hunter in the jungle</u>
Imagine two humans in a jungle. One is an experienced hunter who has lived there his entire life. The other has just arrived and has no experience of living in such a wild environment.

<u>How does this apply to humans? And how can you use it against them?</u>
If asked *"Who would need more food and weapons to feel safe?"*, any human would see that the experienced hunter should need far fewer. And the same goes for any human: The fewer friends, Resources, recognition, etc., he NEEDS, the more secure he is. Humans understand this rationale, but they can't see it applies to their lives.

Again, in the jungle, who do you think is more worried about controlling his surroundings, the experienced hunter who can handle almost any situation or the inexperienced hunter? There is a direct link between a need for control and perceived vulnerability. The fact that some humans NEED to feel in control at all times — omnipotent — is a sign of perceived weakness, just like inexperienced hunters need more food in the jungle. Powerful humans don't need to feel in control; they deal with problems if and when they occur.

Similarly, you can perceive a human who needs lots of approval and can't cope with any rejection as weak and vulnerable.

In severe cases, some humans not only need to control family members' opinions on an important matter, but also those of strangers on issues that are irrelevant. Yes, some humans can get angry if they can't change the views on trivial matters of the most insignificant humans in their lives.

<u>A lust for power — a SYMPTOM</u>
Lust for power is an intense, insatiable desire to control everything — to be all powerful. It happens when a desire (want) for power becomes a

NEED. In this case, no matter how much power he has, a human continually needs more — desperately.

Interestingly, many humans see grand ambitions as positive, but ambitions are only good to certain levels. You see, when a human has a lust for power, he NEEDS incredibly high levels of money and social acceptance to feel safe. And a consequence of extremely high levels of need is that a human's self-image continually sits in the Survival Mode Zone. So, when studied in detail, it's not difficult to realise that the need for control, a lust for power, is a defence mechanism to protect an emotionally vulnerable creature.

We, as hunters, need to invert the link and realise that humans who lust for power are trying to feel safe. Therefore, their unquenchable thirst for power and control is a SYMPTOM, an indication of a disease (a weakness). It exposes a perceived vulnerability, which we can explore.

Interestingly, most humans are unaware of this, and, as a result, you often see them proudly telling others that they are very ambitious and can't wait to achieve success (but they often state this as a NEED, not a want). They are unaware that, depending on how they show that this need matters to them, they could be embarrassing themselves and exposing a weakness.

And, of course, this lust doesn't just relate to power and control. It also applies to vulnerable humans who need excessive amounts of other things, too, like fame, friends, love and social recognition.

***

<u>Tip:</u> An extreme desire to be rich, famous, or popular, is often based on a need to compensate for something else. Look closer.

***

RESOURCES, ALLIANCES & TRUST IN THE CAPTAIN APPLIED

Now, let's look at examples of vulnerable humans needing extra levels of Resources, Alliances and Trust in the Captain to feel safe. We will try to highlight a situation for each of the three needs, but be aware that any situation is usually the result of a combination of needs. For example, as mentioned before, a need for Resources (money) can also relate to a need for Alliances (social approval).

<u>Alliances:</u>
A need for Alliances usually translates as a need for social acceptance, to feel part of a group, to belong and be accepted by a particular tribe. The higher the need for Alliances, the lower a human's self-esteem — the perceived power or confidence he has in himself (related to Trust in the Captain).

You can spot a glaring need for Alliances related to social recognition with humans who crave admiration and friendship from countless people and become nervous at the slightest hint of disapproval from the most insignificant humans in their lives.

Or, a human who needs 100% attention from others *("All the attention in the world means she loves me, and anything less than that is a possible threat")*.

Another example is a human who loses his temper when a single text message is ignored.

You can see a need for Alliances if a human becomes angry when another implies that his success is due to good luck. Yes, some highly successful humans get mad when others suggest that. Why? Well, it indicates that the human needs everyone around him to recognise his capabilities *("It wasn't luck. It was me!")*, so he can feel socially accepted and acknowledged.

Finally, for some humans, a few insults, even from a stranger, can often provoke a quick temper. This reaction also relates to an extreme need for recognition. Yes, even from insignificant strangers. What can we say?

***

<u>Tip:</u> If you can easily rile an animal by questioning his social recognition, you should have no problem defeating it. For you, the best thing that can happen during a hunt is that your prey loses its temper because that is a sign of an irrational being in Survival Mode.

***

If in doubt, what humans call "social media" is a great place to look for vulnerable prey. In this virtual 'sandpit,' socially needy humans are plain to see.

Resources:
We call humans who believe they lack resources "Starving Dogs". One would guess that only mostly impoverished humans need Resources, but this is not always the case. Yes, it is true that the poor can need more money, or a healthier body, to feel well and safe. It's true that many humans on Earth lack the basics for survival.

However, strangely, you will see that some wealthy humans are also desperate for more Resources. And they have a real Starving Dog need, too, not just the Fat Dog kind already discussed. Why? Well, let's say that they create expensive desires, turn them into high levels of debt and then spend their lives worrying about money — desperately chasing the 'steak' like poor people. It's just a bigger steak for a bigger mouth.

By creating mountains of debt, a supposedly 'safe' animal can auto-generate a real need for Resources that otherwise wouldn't exist.

As you can see, the need for Resources isn't necessarily a trait of the poor and downtrodden. You can find it in healthy and wealthy animals, too.

One could say that wealthy humans could need Resources when, for example, they are sick and need to improve their body condition. This scenario is easy to grasp. One could also say that poor humans requiring resources is a 'no-brainer'. However, it seems strange that a wealthy human can be desperate for Resources, like money, to repay a debt, and his desperation is real, not fake, and hidden under insecurity, as we mentioned before.

If you dig deep enough, might you discover his desperation relates to something else? Why has this human put himself in such a predicament? What rational being would auto-generate a need by acquiring an unnecessary asset that he can't afford and then be desperate about the situation?

Perhaps the human sees having a particular asset as a symbol of success that will garner more social approval? After all, given that humans are often insecure and lack self-knowledge, they rely on symbols to prove to themselves and others that they are valuable. Consequently, some Hidden Association, mixed with a lack of self-understanding, can cause a human to desperately need a particular asset.

So, yes, in a case like this, a wealthy human has REAL reasons to be desperate to pay his bills, but the reason for debt-causing acquisitions can relate to a need for Alliances.

<u>Alliances & Resources combined:</u>
As discussed in the first chapters, humans barely grasp the full reality of what is happening around them, so they rely on indicators. Consequently, humans often take relatively small clues to conclude how much another human is worth or deserves attention. These clues could be anything: the family he comes from, what he does for a living or how much money he makes, etc.

As a consequence, humans use this feature to trick the system. How? Well, if small clues can indicate a human's acceptability to others, humans can — and do — manufacture the image they wish to project by creating clues.

Humans manufacture a persona when they flaunt status symbols to increase social acceptance. They can use fancy clothing, jewellery or, maybe, expensive sports cars to encourage others to reach favourable conclusions, to view them as successful human beings.

Therefore, a need for Alliances can easily be confused with a need for Resources because a human with more Resources, like money, will probably be more socially accepted. Make no mistake, though: The luxury goods market comprises a significant portion of consumers who have an enormous need for social acceptance because of low self-confidence.

Of course, you can't determine whether or not your prey is desperate for social approval just by looking at his fancy sports car. Again, the vehicle is but a small sign to take note of, another tip for you to construct assumptions related to the human's Holy Grail and to see if he is desperate and in Survival Mode. So, as usual, it takes time to collect enough data to reach an accurate conclusion.

If you rush, you could head down the 'wrong track'. For example, a human who knows that he must be seen as successful by another human might drive an expensive car to a business meeting to help close a deal. It's not that the human needs the 'bling-mobile' to be confident. Instead, he uses it to convince the other human that he is successful. Got it? So, take your time when observing humans. As usual, what matters are the reasons why they behave in the ways they do.

Therefore, what you must pay attention to is how much a human NEEDS a status symbol to feel good and safe. Ask this question: How comfortable would he be without this symbol? Just like the experienced hunter in the jungle, the more powerful a human is, the fewer requirements he has to feel safe.

So, a craving for status symbols is usually related to a need for respect and social acceptance, which can also result in better access to Resources. It's not the objects these humans seek, but the fulfilment of their basic needs. Objects are a mere means to an end. The tricky part, though, is that humans are oblivious to what's going on, and they confuse status symbols with the goals they seek. As usual, a human's brain uses emotions and desires to play him like a puppet. When humans acquire status symbols, they do, indeed, feel pleasure, and so they believe that the pleasant feelings are because of the object. In fact, it is their brain rewarding them for taking an action that will allow the brain to feel safer. It's as simple as that.

<u>Trust in the Captain:</u>

As you have seen, humans usually compensate for lack of self-esteem with a high need for Resources and Alliances. So, it isn't easy to spot an insecurity (pure Trust in the Captain need) because it can take on several deceptive forms. As a result, you could deduce that there are two major needs to pay attention to: Resources and Alliances. However, we created the Trust in the Captain concept to help you understand the things that frequently influence a human prey's need for Resources and Alliances.

In some cases, though, it is possible to spot some low self-esteem problems that are almost pure. And, interestingly, the signs of insecurity can be misleading. Like, for example, a human who continually NEEDS to overcome a challenge, but he does so for the wrong reasons. This human might be trying to prove (to himself) that he is worthwhile or he might be wishing for others to tell him that he is valuable. As usual, what is important is WHY and HOW MUCH he needs to challenge himself and HOW HE REACTS if he isn't able to do so.

Pure insecurity, though, can be more difficult to spot than other kinds. Like, for example, a human who relishes attending intellectual conferences and having in-depth discussions, but for the wrong reasons.

In such a case, he doesn't enjoy the conversations themselves. What he likes is being the guy who participates in that kind of intellectual activity. So, for this human, he isn't necessarily interested in learning or discovering some truth from a discussion. Instead, he likes speaking esoteric, intellectual gobbledygook because it makes him feel intelligent — superior to others. Do you see how complex human behaviour can be? You must read between the lines.

One way you could expose the human as a 'pointy-head' wannabe is to ask him about the event. If he describes it using pompous and difficult-to-understand language, he may need to feel and look intelligent. With humans like him, their attempts to appear intellectual can be embarrassing and funny. Try to avoid laughing, but you can enjoy the moment.

It is essential for you to know the difference between real and false confidence. Self-confidence should originate from a human's understanding of his abilities and flaws; he will then know what he is or isn't capable of and will rely little on external clues. But, a lack of self-knowledge leads to an excessive reliance on the perception of others and external clues. And this creates a bubble (an extreme level) of a need for Resources and Alliances.

Make no mistake: The only real way for your prey to develop Trust in the Captain is to ... well, be a great Captain, which means having sound abilities and self-knowledge.

EXTERNAL SOURCES OF CONFIDENCE

Pay attention to humans who appear supremely confident and need to show off. The reasons for their 'swagger' are often fake. You see, many humans rely on external entities for self-confidence. It's like a human feeling secure while standing behind two burly security guards. He feels safe because of them, not his abilities. Remove the guards (or make him believe you could), and poof! His peace of mind vanishes.

Some humans use external things, such as money, status symbols, a job title, a partner or a social group, like pillars to help them feel safe. What matters to you, the hunter, is how much a human depends on external things and how vulnerable (and haunted) he will be should they disappear. As a general rule, the more a human relies on external entities, the more he is scared of losing them.

If a human needs to be a millionaire to feel confident, even while retaining millionaire status, he lives in a state of constant anxiety; the idea of losing any part of his wealth is too much to take.

Or, in a case of a jealous human, if he relies on a partner for self-confidence, he can become extremely jealous or desperately in love for the same reason. Rather than a sign of cuteness or love, jealousy indicates insecurity; the human's stability is highly dependent on an external entity (his partner). Usually this insecurity springs from the human not understanding that he needs his partner close by to show him he is loveable, or he needs his partner to feel socially accepted.

We have even observed cases where, for example, a male human is insecure regarding his sexual performance, and his female partner demonstrates approval by having a relationship with him. But, at the moment she leaves, everything falls apart. You see, the male becomes desperate, not because of the broken relationship, but because of the HIDDEN MEANINGS the break up represents: His social approval and self-confidence are broken also. Interesting, don't you think?

Note: The fact that humans overly rely on small indicators to reach deep conclusions about themselves makes things rather dynamic. For example, a human can appear highly confident, but a few months after retiring from the workforce, everything changes. Why? Well, for many humans, work brings a sense of usefulness and purpose, which sustains their self-esteem. Once gone... well, the dearth of positive feedback and recognition that a job can bring can cause their confidence to disappear. So, keep in mind that a human's self-confidence — Trust in the Captain — can change abruptly due to outside events, like losing a job.

So, as always, you must observe the kinds of external things your prey relies on for confidence and the reasons why, which most often boil down to weak leadership on the part of the Captain who lacks self-knowledge.

HOW TO CHOOSE YOUR BAIT?

When hunting humans, the bait must be right. It's like when pursuing a male deer, one of Earth's rudiment animals, you would probably try to attract it with the scent of a doe (female) or specific foods.

When hunting humans, to select the best bait and trap, you must pay attention to how they behave (and consider all previous chapters).

When choosing your bait, what matters the most is whether or not your prey is in Survival Mode and then the REASON for his desperation.

So, always ask these questions: *"Why the overreaction? Why is he nervous or aggressive? What does (he believe) he lack? Does the human see more than just a simple failure? Is there a hidden meaning?"* If you are lucky, the human might even have a strange Allergy to something, like disapproval or a simple word like *failure* or *mistake*.

In all cases, promises and compliments usually work well. Just use the right ones to accommodate what your prey believes it lacks.

Note that, as said already, it is not easy to separate each type of need because they are often intertwined, but let's show some examples of appropriate baits based on different needs.

If a human needs many Alliances to feel safe, compliment and highlight features that will boost his feelings of social approval. For example, tell him he is good looking or well-liked, or whatever (in his culture) increases his social acceptance: *"What white skin!"* or *"Great tan!"* Or, make him feel okay about a weakness, like being too fat, thin, short, tall or dumb. Make it seem unimportant to you, or pretend you haven't noticed. Even if you are lying, he will probably believe you — doing so will give him pleasure. Praising the status symbols a human flaunts can show that they are successfully gaining him more social acceptance.

If your prey needs Resources, promising money now or in the future usually works well. A good job or business opportunity can have the same effect. Sometimes the promise can even be vague because desperate animals are not at all rational. Also, it is worth mentioning that an extreme need for Resources often relates to a perceived lack of power, so doing anything that will make a human feel more powerful, like showing (pretending) he is in control, can be useful, too.

When a human lacks self-confidence, it's like the crew on the ancient ship continually second-guessing their captain's leadership. Not a good situation.

If a human needs self-esteem, you can use the right compliments (to reinforce some specific abilities or skills he may have) to play with what matters to him and with what he is insecure about. The difference to Alliances, here, is that, for a self-esteem issue, it is more useful to praise your prey's achievements and compliment him directly, NOT his external entities (such as status symbols he might flaunt). Praising his status symbols is like complimenting the bodyguards around him. Instead, tell the human that it is he who is strong, and imply that he doesn't need bodyguards for protection.

Another approach that works well with a human lacking self-esteem is to set a challenge he can handle. Some small mission that you know will be difficult enough for him to be proud of achieving. Just make sure he succeeds — even help him if necessary. And, of course, praise the human for his accomplishment: *"Good job!"* Things like that usually work. After all, the problem here is the insecure Captain inside his head, not the Resources or Alliances. Help the Captain earn the respect of his Crew.

***

<u>Tip:</u> As a rule, the happier a human is with a compliment, the more he needs it. And the more he needs external reinforcement, the more insecure he is. So, if your prey enjoys compliments a little too much, he will often be an easy target.

***

CONCLUSIONS

So, extreme nervousness, hate and anger, etc., equate to vulnerability, which means a human lacks one or more of the three fundamental needs. The animal feels he is in danger.

It can't get any simpler: The brain identifies a lack of something it believes is essential and then creates a range of unpleasant feelings, such as fear, anxiety, anger, hate, or even aggression, to compel the animal to move quickly to fix the problem.

It works with a PERCEIVED need, not necessarily an ACTUAL need. And, the more humans need something, the easier it is to scare them.

To keep things simple, the two crucial needs to observe are

Resources and Alliances. However, both are highly dependent on Trust in the Captain.

Prey in Survival Mode is always preferable because they lose their capacity to think clearly. Ideally, your prey should be in this state during a hunt. After all, when in battle, the best thing that can happen is for your enemy to lose his temper because, when he does, he is far more likely to make desperate moves and stupid mistakes. The last thing you want to hunt is a rational creature that can calmly choose the best options. You need to be able to create and impose fear and point to the only escape route, where your trap will be waiting.

So, pay attention to when and why a human loses his temper. And when he does, consider whether he faces a real threat or if it is just an overreaction from a cornered and scared animal. We, as hunters, are especially fond of overreactions because they expose an increased vulnerability.

The key is always to scratch the surface to unearth what need the prey seeks and how it tries to get it (Hidden Associations — the meanings behind). This way you will be able to prepare suitable bait using the little clues that lead to final statements in a human's head.

And don't worry. Even if all these tactics seem obvious, they should still work because animals in fight-or-flight mode don't see much; they are not rational beings

In the next chapter, we will explore a few practical cases to make it easier for you to spot an animal in Survival Mode.

14

FEAR

PRACTICAL TIPS

As a novice hunter, you should start with extra-vulnerable prey — those that need to feel omnipotent all the time. These humans despise feeling any lack of power. Not surprisingly, they always lose their temper because, of course, they are not that powerful, and life, in one way or another, continually reminds them of the fact. Consequently, these humans are always in Survival Mode, PERMANENTLY on edge, and easy to scare and manipulate.

Let's show a practical example of a human slipping into Survival Mode due to an unnecessary situation.

ANGER AS A SIGN OF WEAKNESS
An example

When a wealthy company owner fires an employee for causing a financial loss (but nothing major), if he presents signs of anger and aggression (becomes irate and shouts at the employee), that is a sign of weakness.

Okay, the employee's mistake might have led to losses, but a strong captain needn't express big emotions to deal with problems. As a hunter, you must always ask, *"What does it (the situation, the object, etc.) mean for this angry human being?"*

Why the boss feels like he is in Survival Mode doesn't matter as much as the fact that he IS in Survival Mode. However, let's speculate that he feels threatened because an employee's mistake might expose him as a poor manager who lacks judgement when hiring staff. Maybe he needs to show everyone in the office that he is a 'big man' to compensate for his perceived lack of control? An unsatisfactory homelife may drive him to feel the need to impose his power on a weak victim. There are many possible reasons, all of which will lead to the boss feeling vulnerable and needing to fight back like a cornered animal.

If the boss perceived himself as powerful and confident, why would he waste energy shouting at his employee? Well, he wouldn't. Instead, he would calmly tell the employee to clear his desk. The rule can't get any simpler: An animal that loses its temper is vulnerable.

Some other common signs that identify vulnerable prey are:
1.   Obsessions — an escape to a new world
2.   Extreme niceness — a slave of acceptance
3.   Extreme Truths — a search for certainty
4.   Drugs — relief by ignoring bad results

OBSESSIONS
An escape to a new world

Pay attention because sometimes emotions that humans display can be 'over the top' — excessive — for a situation: suffering too much or being excessively happy, for example. These discrepancies provide opportunities for the hunter. One typical cause of over-the-top emotions is an obsession.

How to spot the problem?

Look for extreme passions in sport, work, gambling, video games, hobbies — even a personal project (such as writing a book). Imagine how a human would react to the hint that there is a chance he will be deprived of what he loves for a few days. If he gets desperate or nervous, you might have struck gold — an easy weakness, an obsession.

An obsession often begins when a human feels he lacks something fundamental: Alliances, the need to feel significant, etc. And he could compensate for this perceived deficiency with, for example, a virtual life where he receives social recognition and acceptance. The pleasure of a new life can quickly become an obsession.

Check it out for yourself: For some obsessive creatures, 30 seconds without the internet can seem like 30 minutes without oxygen. Don't believe us? Pull the plug and watch them turn blue.

Another example is a human who is obsessed with a sports team to the point that it becomes his life. He could be compensating for a weakness. How? Well, perhaps he needs to feel important (Alliances), so he fulfils this need with the camaraderie he enjoys when supporting a team. When he is with his mates (his group), he feels powerful; he sees the victories of his team while his life has very few to celebrate. By supporting his team he compensates for the problems in his life. And when his support becomes extreme, it is an obsession. His tribe becomes his life. In this case, a threat to his team (a loss) could lead the human directly to Survival Mode — as if his life were under threat. Again, you see here a situation where a human uses an external entity to fulfil a basic need, and so he becomes more vulnerable to threats.

Check it out for yourself: You should see obsessive sports fans when their team loses a match. They look like desperate soldiers battling for their lives. It's quite funny, actually; they *really do* feel threatened. Just keep a distance because they often 'bite'.

Note: This doesn't apply just to sports. The 'tribe' mentioned above can be almost any kind of division: race, gender, political views, religion, etc. For humans, being part of a group can bring immense pleasure because it makes them feel powerful. And, if they need the group too much, it can become an obsession.

Work, too, can be a source of obsession. Like when a human with an unhappy homelife strives for recognition and importance at his job to compensate, to the point that he becomes obsessed.

<u>Check it out for yourself</u>: For a human, one sick-day at home could be extremely stressful. Again, watch his reactions to small problems. Although there is no threat, he is stressed. How curious?

And let's not even discuss criticising a human's project, like a book, of which he is obsessed. Oh, boy … he'll feel as if there is an attack on his child!

Examples of over-the-top emotions are endless, and you can only guess the causes because, for each obsession, you can draw an infinite number of bridges in a human's mind. As a rule, any overreaction to a situation usually links to a weakness that is far bigger than what appears on the surface.

EXTREMELY NICE HUMANS
Slaves of acceptance

Too angry is obvious, but too nice? Yes, both extreme behaviours are signs of which to pay attention. Here, though, we will talk about, often misunderstood, extremely nice humans. You know, those do-gooders who never complain and always make sacrifices to help others?

These humans you must observe with care because individuals who feel they have met their basic needs can display altruistic behaviour, and so they pursue a Holy Grail that happens to be useful to society. After all, giving to (helping) others when a human is already 'full' inside makes sense; he's okay inside, and so he wants to help others — he doesn't need the basics anymore. Doing good gives the human pleasure because he is nearing his Holy Grail, super-self (after being fulfilled, not before).

Don't be misguided, though. Interestingly, some humans can behave like Mother Teresa (one of Earth's most famous do-gooders) and still be empty inside. What do we mean? Well, lacking minimum levels of one or more basic requirements or, in other words, operating in Survival Mode. It's like humans with low self-esteem (Trust in the Captain) who accept situations similar to slavery (being extremely good to anyone and taking humiliation without fighting back). If a human is too kind to everyone, look deeply because you might find a useful clue. It could be that he craves social approval to reach a minimum level of self-esteem.

Of course, we must separate 'full' humans who help others (and hardly get nervous) because they find pleasure in doing so, to those who are in Survival Mode and will dive into any charitable situation to fulfil their need for social approval.

In the case of humans in Survival Mode who do good, they usually do so because there is no alternative; they have a fundamental need to fulfil, and the only way to do that is to help others. These humans do good because, inside, they are empty and begging to become full.

So, humans who are nice all the time, the ones with high morals who can't say no to anyone, are more likely to be cowardly, weak and seeking social approval. They do good and like to brag about the fact. However, they are 'so nice', not because they don't want to tear the wings off flies, but most often because they don't think they have it in them to do so. They use their incapacity, lack of 'claws', to their advantage. Rather than being 'whiter than the driven snow', they are just hopeless.

It's worth pointing out that there are reasons for excessively pleasant behaviour other than a need for acceptance — like a need to compete. You see, the actions of 'slaves of acceptance' are often also mingled with a need to feel superior to others — better than the rest of humanity — even if this means being humiliated. As odd as it sounds, in these cases, humans can compete to be the nicest.

Regardless of the reason for the extreme behaviour, you must determine whether a human is full or empty, which is what matters. Observe and try to work out the source for his extremely nice behaviour. As a hunter, you must learn to separate full and empty do-gooder animals.

EXTREME TRUTHS
A search for certainty

Among humans, doubt is a luxury that very few can afford. As mentioned in the chapter *Hidden Associations*, humans don't usually cope well with uncertainty due to its association with danger. Naturally, humans in Survival Mode hate unpredictability and do anything to avoid it. Any kind of unknown can be uncomfortable for them, so they fight back by creating 'truths' for what they don't understand. However, these humans can be misleading because their black-and-white statements of truth are often confused with confidence when, in fact, they can be signs of a vulnerable animal in Survival Mode that can't cope with uncertainty.

You see, some humans take avoidance of uncertainty to extreme levels and side-step the unknown entirely. And the fact that the unknown is intrinsic to humans' lives makes things tricky. Let's look at some more ways to spot vulnerable prey.

<u>An answer for the afterlife</u>: Some humans will often state, with 100% certainty, and with no room for doubt, that there is or isn't an afterlife. Sure, humans can believe whatever they like, but failing to realise that a belief is an assumption and not a final truth is a sign of weakness — an Allergy to uncertainty and unpredictability. Of course, no human knows for sure what happens when they die.

So, to clarify, your prey can believe in many theories or scenarios for life after death: once dead, humans disappear forever, or that life, for some reason, is a simulation, etc. However, few acknowledge that, in fact, they don't know for sure. And if a human can't allow uncertainty, this is an encouraging sign for the hunter.

Surprisingly, even smart humans step into this trap. Scientists, for example, often state with conviction that there is no afterlife. And, even though they are among Earth's elite, for them, too, it's impossible to know for sure. They also need to anchor themselves in certainty.

<u>Origins of everything</u>: Denying scientists' discoveries of evolution of the species, and the colossal explosion (the "Big Bang", as they call it) that 'kicked off' life, doesn't seem smart. However, it should be obvious to scientists that nobody actually knows for sure how, out of nothing, life popped up on Earth, or what happened before the Big Bang. And, yet, they often state that they have found the complete truth about the history of the universe.

Let's take the origins of life for example. The best explanation scientists have for how life came about sounds like magic. They say that, from nothing, and under certain conditions, that somehow some dead stuff became alive and created a cell, and at some point, this cell magically survived and acquired the ability to reproduce.

Weird, wouldn't you say? It is true that, for now, this explanation is the best scientists can come up with. Fair enough. However, it should be apparent to them that it falls far short of being a final statement. And, if scientists don't know this, how can they state for sure that there is nothing before or after life? Haha! Of course, nobody knows with certainty how the world as we know it began. So, even for brilliant humans, it is difficult to understand that their theories start with assumptions.

***

Even if you hear a human say (like we heard from one of Earth's highly intelligent professors), *"Neither life or the universe has meaning. That's the truth. Get over it!"* Don't worry; he is also trying to escape uncertainty — just like the believers.

***

Most humans seek answers to questions about God or the laws of physics. They are desperate to avoid uncertainty, regardless of the explanations they find. And, of course, no answer can, without doubt, explain everything about the beginning of the universe, life or the mystery of existence.

<u>Controversial issues</u>: As a hunter, you can spot extreme cases of vulnerable humans by asking open questions about controversial issues, like marriage, morality or the meaning of life. Take note of humans who are closed to any sign of doubt and are full of rules for how to live life and its meaning (particularly if the subject makes them nervous); they are usually vulnerable because they are either incapable of seeing an alternative view or, most often, too afraid to recognise that they don't know the answer to an issue.

<u>Note</u>: Considering what we said about religion in the chapters about the Holy Grail will be useful for you here. You see, religion removes doubts related to the meaning of life, morals, acceptable behaviour and life after death, etc. What a deal! Regardless of whether it's true or not, a human's religion brings a lot of relief.

Finally, there is another crutch that vulnerable humans lean on: drugs.

DRUGS
Relief by ignoring bad results

For humans, a good strategy for easing anxiety when an aeroplane is falling from the sky is to avoid looking out the window: *"If I can't see it, I don't have to worry."* At least, that seems to be the rationale for some humans when dealing with problems in their lives.

You see, like the Weak Captain, where blame and denial help him feel safe, humans can create alternative realities by consuming substances that lower their capacity to think about and judge a situation.

Check out this behaviour because it's intriguing: To deal with the problems they face, many humans consume drugs. We won't discuss the different types here, rather the concept and the usual reasons for using them.

The most popular drug is alcohol. And how does it work? Well, alcohol affects judgement, so humans are less capable of evaluating whether or not they are below the minimum levels of need. Naturally, especially when in Survival Mode, alcohol brings relief.

It is like the captain wearing earplugs to avoid listening to complaints from his crew. It's easy to see how blocking one's ears can bring short-term relief; however, doing so will, of course, never fix a problem.

Not all humans use drugs to block out problems. Some take them for recreational purposes and in moderation. What matters for you is the frequency, amount and, most importantly, the reason a human takes drugs — the *real* reason, not what he tells you. Hardly any human will say that it is because he is too weak to cope with life's 'slings and arrows'. So, you must rely on your skills of observation to uncover the truth.

Spoiler alert: It is true that not all humans who partake in drugs are weak. However, given the vast majority of them are below the minimum requirements to feel safe, that they operate in Survival Mode, we think you can guess the reason for getting high in the vast majority of cases.

We can even state that the majority of humans, most of the time, are only satisfied and happy when reminiscing about the past (usually as better than it was) or when they cancel (or minimise) their capacity for judgement (when intoxicated) to see their terrible Survival Mode situation.

Yes, that is quite a strong statement, but based on our vast experience as hunters, true none the less. As you have seen, humans continually transform wants into needs. Consequently, they are usually in Survival Mode and often take drugs to minimise the unfortunate situations of which they continuously get themselves into, or to escape by remembering the past as better than it was, or hoping for a future far better than it will be — all tactics to escape the dark reality of living in Survival Mode.

<u>Now, you do the maths:</u> Consider all of the above — how often humans lose their temper, their obsessions, need for certainty, use of drugs, extreme need for money and social acceptance. Then, observe. Do most humans live in (almost) permanent Survival Mode or not?!

Part V is about humans' lack of self-knowledge and the reasons, which you will find are not straightforward, but fascinating nonetheless. We also show why even if a human were to read this book, he would still often be haunted by the same problems again and again.

PART V
SECRETS BEHIND HUMAN
IGNORANCE

15

PRELUDE

THE FOUR CHARACTERISTICS

So, why can't humans fix the problems discussed in this book? Why are they most often in Survival Mode? Why are they unaware of their Hidden Associations and their Drawers? Why can't humans form a clear picture of the Holy Grail they pursue? It's hard to believe that rational beings would face the same old problems time and again without knowing, right?

Well, it happens. And the answer, whether you believe it or not, is that most humans suffer from an acute lack of self-knowledge. And if this isn't obvious to you, this prelude and the next two chapters (which are interconnected) will demonstrate the fact.

We need to ensure that you're adequately prepared, so let's examine four characteristics of the human mind: comparison, adaptability, judgement and Rigid Rules.

When all four are combined and applied (which we do in the following chapters), things become interesting. However, first, let's look at each characteristic individually.

COMPARISON

To determine whether their situation is good or bad — whether they are a winner or loser — humans compare themselves to others. Which sounds reasonable, right? The problem, though, is that they rely too much on comparisons that are flawed, narrow and short-term. Humans can barely see the big picture. They usually compare themselves to the nearby 'herd' — which could be heading in either the right direction or straight into the jaws of a crocodile.

It's like an athlete who doesn't know if he's running in the right marathon. Regardless, he checks to see if he is ahead or behind the runners around him. Whether or not he's running in the right direction — or race — is beside the point.

And, one way to compare is to compete, so humans compete a lot — much more than is necessary — in discussions, relationships and between friends, etc.

ADAPTABILITY

Like clay, humans are malleable and can adapt to almost any situation. This characteristic may make them seem formidable, and they are. However, bear in mind that because humans will almost always adjust to a circumstance, good or bad, their minimum requirements to feel safe continually rise, and so their ongoing problems persist.

Here's an example: Give hot water to a human who has only ever experienced cold showers, and after a few months, he won't be able to imagine life without this new luxury. Hot water will become a NEED and the new standard. The same applies to things like jobs, houses and partnerships. Consequently, many prey, who should be in a good, safe situation, are often in Survival Mode. Priceless!

JUDGEMENT

Humans judge. Get over it.

Given you have reached this point in our book, you'll know that many associations and decisions about, for example, in which Drawer to place information, happen at Crew level, before the Captain gets involved. Consequently, humans can't fully control their feelings and prejudices.

And, humans don't understand this fact. Here's an example of what we mean: During your time on Earth, you will likely hear humans say, *"Don't judge."* Well, if they followed our rationale, they would say, *"I know you can't fully control how you judge things, but your Captain should be wise enough to pay attention and question the information he receives. So, question your judgements to avoid wrong actions."*

However, given that humans have no idea about how their central system works, they tell others not to judge — like as if humans could actually fully control their thoughts and desires.

***

The key concept to understand here is that most judgements humans make happen BEFORE they are AWARE that they are judging.

***

Let's now look at the last concept.

RIGID RULES

Humans judge and place things into categories all the time. And to help with their judgements, they formulate sets of moral standards — internal laws. Naturally, humans judge others based on the standards they create, and those who fail to comply are "undesirable", "enemies" or "losers".

One common, simple rule is that humans shouldn't be rude to others. One should work hard is another. Simple stuff. But humans' laws can be stricter, more specific, and even dictate the minimum amount of success or wealth a human must achieve to be a winner, or what one should or shouldn't desire (like homosexuality is wrong).

Yes, humans judge others on things that no human can FULLY control, such as desires and thoughts. For a human, the more rigid and specific his rules are, the harder it is for those around him to comply and, funnily enough, the more "losers" and "enemies" seem to surround him. In fact, a human's moral requirements can become so severe that almost no one meets the grade.

So, those are the four characteristics: <u>comparison, adaptability, judgement and Rigid Rules.</u>

Simple, aren't they? But wait! There is a trick.

THE DETAIL THAT CHANGES EVERYTHING

Until now, we've explained the Rigid Rules as internal standards to judge OTHER humans. However, this is not the full story.

The backlash for a human with Rigid Rules is that he also applies them to himself, which creates a sequence of problems.

Things have just become interesting, don't you think?

In the next chapter, armed with this background information, we will delve deeper into Rigid Rules and see what happens when a human points a 'gun', not just at others, but also at himself.

16

BUILDING A CAGE
THE SURVEILLANCE SYSTEM

From childhood to adulthood, a human creates rules for behaving in society — moral standards learned from parents, religion, those in authority and even other kids at school, etc. The result is a 'guide to life' with contributions from every human who has ever tried to make him behave.

Remember, humans are born into an 'alien world'.

So, rules help them understand what is right or wrong, desirable or undesirable, within their social group; they are a moral conscience to help humans control their instincts. Don't misunderstand us. There is nothing wrong with rules; obviously, humans must forgo some of their animalistic urges to get along in a civilised society.

For example:

- *"I can't have the other kid's toy just because I want it."*
- *"I can't rape that human just because I want sex."*
- *"I can't kill that human because he annoyed me."*

Obvious stuff, right?

And how do Rigid Rules control human behaviour? Like a personal judge, they make humans feel guilt and shame. Rules reward with pride and happiness when obeyed, and punish with shame and remorse when disobeyed. So, failing to comply with his Rigid Rules can make a human feel guilty, ashamed, stupid — like a loser. All that stuff.

Are humans aware of their Rigid Rules? No. The vast majority are unclear at the Captain level and they can feel guilt and remorse without fully understanding why. Like a human's Holy Grail, Hidden Associations and minimum requirements to feel safe, a large portion of his Rigid Rules are at the Crew level, so his Captain is not fully aware they exist.

<u>Note</u>: Wait! But all of this resembles what we discussed in the *Holy Grail* and *Survival Mode* chapters. Why are we discussing Rigid Rules as a new characteristic? Well, indeed, the three are all interconnected, but us clearly explaining Rigid Rules here should help you to understand how they prevent humans from investigating their thoughts and desires. You will see.

Anyway, continuing …

It starts with little things such as, *"I am not allowed to be jealous of my little brother. He is family,"* even though it is perfectly reasonable for a child not to like sharing his parents' attention, at least when his new sibling first arrives. But a human's Rigid Rules don't allow for jealously within families. It's wrong, forbidden. So, what does the older child do? Well, he can't bear being jealous of his little brother (it's unacceptable according to his interpretation of his parents' Rigid Rules), so, as time passes by, he learns not to address the issue and to hide his feelings. Consequently, the human often becomes angry at other things while unaware that the real source of his ire is his repressed feelings.

And, in case you are wondering, no, it doesn't stop when humans are kids. Remember in the *Brain's Puppet* chapter the extreme example of a human who moved to a new country because he can't stand competing with his sister, even though he often feels homesick? The same rationale applies there and in so many other situations — like the hatred humans can feel for those they claim to love.

Now, imagine how crazy things can get if, somewhere at the Crew level, a human has Rigid Rules like these:
- *"I am not allowed to be rejected by anyone."* A being with a

high need for social approval is created. Remember the Slaves of Acceptance? Those humans who are desperate to please and fit in?

- *"I am not allowed to have doubts or not to know something."* The holder of the truth, who can't accept any conflicting reality or uncertainty, is born.
- *"I am not allowed to have flaws or make mistakes."* The perfectionist is created, who pretty much has a high need for everything and who, not surprisingly, will often either deny or overreact to the slightest sign of a flaw or mistake.
- *"I am not allowed to come second place."* The desperately competitive human is created. Winning becomes an obsession.

As mentioned, a human's Rigid Rules can become complicated and narrow concerning the minimum wealth required to be a winner, when to marry, the desirable body shape, the right skin colour, whom one can or can't desire or hate, what dreams are acceptable … the list is endless.

Yes! Even desires! Rigid Rules can also dictate what humans should think about or yearn for.

***

<u>Tip:</u> In the case of overly competitive humans, you can always spend time theorising about and investigating the situation. But if you want to 'cut to the chase', here you go: Look deeply, and more often than not you will find that these hugely competitive creatures are in a never-ending quest to prove to Daddy that:

A. They are worthy of love
B. Daddy is wrong, or
C. They are better than Daddy

Things like that.

So, whenever you see this kind of human, the relationship between him and his parents should be a good starting point to look for weaknesses and insecurities that cause abnormal behaviour.

***

THE DRAGON INSIDE THE HUMAN MIND

<u>Tell a human this story: Afraid of the Dragons in the dark</u>
Imagine a castle with scary, dark dungeons. Housed within these dank chambers, are monstrous, fire-breathing dragons, each holding secrets that could potentially dethrone the king. The king wants to keep his throne, of course. So, he never dares to set foot in the dungeons and forbids everyone else from going there as well.

<u>How does this apply to humans? And how can you use it against them?</u>
Like a king can fear dungeons — and what they contain — humans are often afraid of their thoughts and desires, so instead of trying to understand them, they block them out.

Humans don't investigate what's going on in their minds because, quite frankly, they're terrified of what they might find. With so many Rigid Rules to comply with, their thoughts and desires are like personal dragons.

Think of it like this: What would you do if one of the rooms in your house (you don't know which) concealed a dragon? Would you explore them all to track down the fire-breathing horror or stay put in the sanctuary of the one room you knew was safe? Well, when it comes to humans, most choose the latter. And, they do so their entire lives.

As a consequence, humans are not masters of their minds. Instead, they are their Brain's Puppets and react to emotions and desires with no understanding of why.

NO RISKY INVESTIGATION ALLOWED

It's not the darkness that scares humans. No, they fear what it conceals.

For example, a human can't allow himself to find the slightest clue that may resemble jealousy or envy towards close family. Or, he can feel guilty about noticing the beauty of a human of the same sex (even if he feels no sexual attraction). The human can't risk discovering a clue that he may have had a 'forbidden thought'. Even for a second.

Humans judge themselves by their Rigid Rules, and so they are too afraid to investigate their minds because they can't afford to stumble upon unexpected 'wrong' thoughts and desires.

For a human, what's the solution? Ignore what he's thinking, of course, and be haunted for life. Brilliant! And, as time goes by, thoughts and desires don't disappear, and repression fuels them like oxygen does a flame.

However, let us make it clear: Humans don't repress thoughts and desires because they want to. Rather, they do so because not complying with their internal rules is too problematic, unbearable. For the majority of humans there is no other solution but to ignore what they think and feel. Using our favourite ship metaphor, to protect the captain, the messenger represses the message because the captain can't take the truth.

Let's look at a practical application in a severe case like the perfectionist mentioned earlier.

THE BACKLASH OF PERFECTIONISM
When "I am not allowed to have flaws or make mistakes"
is an inner rule.

Some humans try to live life under the glaze of perfection, and their lives HAVE TO look perfect. Don't be intimidated, though. Most often a need for perfection is a weakness born from ignorance about themselves and those around them.

For humans who pursue perfection all the time, life is often a nightmare because they NEED to be perfect. Note that such a need relates to extremely high minimum requirements (which perfection-seeking humans confuse with their Holy Grail) to feel safe. The mission is a NEED, not a goal. These humans have to be a super version of themselves. All the time. Needing to be perfect is an extremely rigid inner rule, and such humans can't make any mistakes or face life's hurdles. Show a perfection-seeking human a single flaw, and he will most likely deny it and become desperate. Too easy.

Remember in the *Drawers* chapter the world-champion female fighter who, unbelievably, considered committing suicide after she suffered her first defeat? She NEEDED to be the champion. Can you see the nightmare this NEED, this extremely Rigid Rule, can cause?

Humans who pretend to live an idyllic life and brag about it often have Rigid Rules of which to comply. Everything seems brilliant on the surface, but these humans live a nightmare and continuously fear the possibility of discovering a mistake or flaw. The bar for 'perfect' humans is so high that they spend every ounce of energy trying to reach it.

And, there are other consequences. You see, a perfection-seeking human's Rigid Rules often apply to others, too. Imagine the pressure on family and friends — particularly partners and children. After all, a perfect human can't afford, for example, an imperfect child, can he?

Also, imagine what it's like mating with these humans. Do you think they would go easy on a partner if his performance was anything but perfect? Would a perfection-seeking human accept a flaw? No, you guessed it right; rather than just enjoying the moment, mating is a chance to prove stuff to themselves. They bring the judge to bed. *"You better do it right, boy..."* Haha!

What most humans don't realise is that those who always need to present themselves as highly successful most often constantly judge themselves whether they really are perfect. Consequently, they are usually unable to explore their Dungeons because, without a doubt, there will be conflicting thoughts and weaknesses — Dragons — lurking there.

So, tear off the mask of perfectionism and, most often, you will look into the eyes of a terrified soul living the never-ending nightmare of HAVING to be perfect ALL the time because *"That's what Daddy wants."* Though usually unaware, at the Crew level, these humans often are afraid of discovering that they are imposters.

Incredibly, even a small 'nefarious' thought can send 'perfect' humans to the Loser Drawer. So, they constantly repress anything that fails to comply with their Rigid Rules. ALL of them. *"Not one flaw, please! I can't cope with it."*

ALIENATION FROM INSTINCTS

So, humans often can't live up to their moral requirements because of their severity. Their rules dictate that they be something they are not. Think about it. All humans, including the most pious, are still, deep down, animals with instincts. Eventually, all humans have forbidden thoughts and desires that are so threatening that they must be repressed.

Now, think about the complexity of the human mind, all the wild Hidden Associations and infinite possibilities. How many 'wrong' thoughts can humans have that, if ignored, will continue to influence their lives? Remember the student who gets nervous when making a simple class presentation because he links performance and success to being accepted and loved by his parents? If he can't acknowledge why he is afraid, the fear will most likely continue to haunt him.

If humans use blame and denial to cope with situations, their nefarious thoughts will stick around, make noise — whether repressed or not. No human can fix a forbidden thought or desire by ignoring it. And the more rigid humans' inner rules are, the more things become taboo, and humans become increasingly alienated from their instincts and inner truths.

CONCLUSIONS

So, one reason for humans' ignorance is clear: Once they set Rigid Rules, facing their Dungeons, which may conceal noncompliant thoughts and desires — Dragons — is too horrifying. Hence, no internal investigation is allowed.

17

OBSERVE THE QUARRY
TIME & RESILIENCE

An average human being would consider himself to be the king of his Castle (his mind). Fair enough. More often than not, though, mainly due to incompetence, humans are far from being their own masters. They resemble clown kings, impotent rulers governed by dark forces that they are too afraid to face, even acknowledge.

An odd way to begin this chapter? You will see….

As always, there is no better way to explain a concept than to present an example.

<u>Tell a human this story: The weird date with a stranger</u>

Imagine a human who wants to get to know another. However, he never really spends time with her. The pair may, for example, go to the cinema together, but they never actually talk or listen to each other. He pays absolutely no attention to his date. After years of going out (without conversing with or paying attention to his companion), the human is surprised that he doesn't have a clue about who the other human really is.

<u>How does this apply to humans? And how can you use it against them?</u>
Most humans would think this story is stupid, but they don't realise that it mirrors their lives.

You see, humans understand that to get to know another human being, they must spend time with them. What they can't quite get, though, is that the same applies to their minds. Without paying attention to what is going on inside, a human will not get to know himself. And, if humans realised how little they know about themselves, they'd be astonished.

In general, humans follow the path below:

One
OUTWARD LOOKING

Humans spend their lives looking outwards and repressing dark thoughts. These animals never reflect; they don't want to encounter ideas they will have to suppress, so they prefer not to look.

Humans search for novelties and try to keep busy during work and their spare time because they can't bear the idea of spending time alone doing nothing. That's a nightmare.

Humans hate looking within — consciousness is a 'disease' that brings an excessive burden. So, they flee from conflicting thoughts by using distractions and external symbols to provide assurance that they are worthwhile beings. These human animals try to protect themselves from the despair of unwelcome ideas, instincts and 'inconvenient' truths. The fear of confronting their Dragons is so mortifying that many humans can't sit alone, even for just a few minutes, without a distraction. This lack of internal investigation is the cause of enormous ignorance.

Two
INNER IGNORANCE

Humans claim they find pleasure by looking outwards (taking on hobbies, keeping busy), and, indeed, they do. Usually not for the reasons they claim, though. The real pleasure from outward looking comes from avoiding inner darkness.

With all that said, how vulnerable is an army or a sports team, if it doesn't know its weak links and so can't prepare to overcome them? Turning a blind eye just leaves more room for opponents to explore. Denial is not a smart strategy, yet it is one most humans subscribe to.

Humans usually refuse to look inwards to understand who they are, their thoughts, what they need and want. Consequently, they have no idea about whether or not they are valuable. Humans never become complete beings (aware of their good and bad sides: skills, desires, flaws, dark thoughts, Holy Grail, Hidden Associations, Drawers). And, given this refusal to look inwards, to feel complete and confident, they play with what they have: comparison.

Three
EXCESSIVE COMPARISON & ADAPTATION

Yes, as a consequence of ignoring what happens inside, humans rely excessively on comparison to analyse their situation. *"Am I a winner or a loser? No idea. Let me compare myself with you and you and you...."*

Because of over reliance on comparison, humans also compete excessively, as if their lives were a battle of life and death, to test their limits (they need to win to feel safe). By competing, humans regularly check if they are acceptable beings. Remember the high need for Alliances?

Interestingly, because of humans' excessive use of comparison, they adapt to almost any situation. Good or bad. Of course, one may think that such an ability should be a good thing. However, humans usually use their adaptability to their disadvantage. And if this isn't clear yet, it soon will be.

You see, no matter what humans have, they can still be in Survival Mode because any new luxury or success soon becomes the new standard of which they must maintain.

"Got a fantastic new job? Flying business class now? Dating the love of your life?" It doesn't matter; all these wins will become the new minimum standard (a need) of which a human can't lose or that he must improve on.

Don't believe us? Give a human a dishwasher and observe his behaviour over the next few weeks. Soon after receiving the appliance, he will be unable to imagine a life without it. The dishwasher will become the new standard. *"I can never wash dishes by hand again, ever! It would be the end of my world if I had to!"* Haha!

Now, imagine the other stuff humans can adapt to and that you can play with.

The rationale seems to be, *"Am I in a good or bad situation? I don't know. All I know is whether it is better than yours or whether or not it has improved from a few months ago."* Often, that's the only comparison humans make.

As a consequence of their adaptability, humans can behave like desperate, cornered animals in almost any situation, good or bad. Even the very rich often act this way because rather than comparing themselves with what THEY want to achieve, they compare themselves with other wealthy humans. Wealthy humans also easily transform wants into needs and become anxious when they don't get them — *"I'm losing to the competition!"*

So, humans adapt and, even when in an extremely good situation, are often in Survival Mode because they refuse to look inwards to analyse adequately how good or bad their life is. All they can do is compare their current situation to the past and to other humans.

Humans' minimal skills of comparison

Yes, humans compare a lot. Comparison, though, is often superficial because humans' capacity to consider data for thorough analysis is often limited. They can usually only see a short distance into the past or future to make comparisons of themselves, for example.

This is funny (tragic for them). Humans often consider themselves lucky if they survive a car accident with only a few scratches. They forget that the lucky ones are those who weren't in the crash in the first place. You see, these car-crash survivors compare things that are close and reach the conclusion that they are lucky.

The same applies to health. Humans will be happy that they are healthy after recently overcoming an illness. However, those who have not been ill lately generally don't appreciate that they are in good health.

Poor reflection, high levels of comparison and excessive adaptation equal "set-to-fail", a formula that explains why today, even though humans live better than kings of days gone by, most are still permanently in Survival Mode.

Humans can hardly see far beyond where they are now (their *real* current situation), and improvements in their lives won't change much. They just become a new standard, and, consequently, it's usually easy to scare humans, regardless of how good their lives are.

Adaptation applied:

In our experience, it takes most humans several months to adapt to major life transformations, but they eventually get there. After a short while, the new situation becomes a reality because the human can't see far backwards and forwards in time. *"Am I better than I was a few months ago?"* seems to be the question.

So, humans compare a lot to see where they are and then adapt. Often, a few months is the maximum a human can reflect on to decide whether his situation is good or otherwise.

It's not easy for hunters to understand this human feature, so we will explain.

In these two examples, regardless of whether your prey's life improves (earns more money) or deteriorates (suffers ill health), most often, after some time, the new situation will become his reality of which he uses to compare how well he is doing in life.

After a while, a human who enjoys a sudden financial windfall will consider his situation (being rich) to be his new standard. Additional money just raises his minimum requirement for Resources, and he suffers should he sink below it.

The human can't see the whole spectrum, just a short period forwards or backwards. So, even though he has more money than he would dare to dream of a few years ago, he can still sink into depression and anxiety.

On the other hand, let's consider a human who just had an accident. He will suffer because for some time he will be far from his Holy Grail and most likely also in Survival Mode. After all, the human is now partially disabled. However, after a few months, some humans reallocate their Holy Grail to something more realistic for their new situation and adjust their minimum requirements. They begin to compare from a new starting point.

Consequently, after some time, a human who suffered an accident and became disabled can feel better than one who is in perfect health.

Even more than the newly rich human? Yes, the disabled human can adjust his Holy Grail, lower his minimum requirements to feel safe and start feeling like he's moving forward while the rich human feels stuck in the same position or sliding backwards. All this happens because humans adapt without making significant reflections, without taking a long-term view, and they rely excessively on comparisons that are superficial, flawed, narrow and short-term.

In the examples above, the disabled human is more satisfied with life than the wealthy one. Remember, humans are creatures of pleasure, and the disabled human is getting more of it. So, as a hunter, of the two, it is often easier to play with the fears of the anxious, wealthy prey.

<u>Curiosity</u>: On Earth, there is a group of humans that is well aware of how the human mind works and recognises that humans often rely too much on comparison. These humans are called "marketers" and they, for example, quite often use consumers' overreliance on comparison to trick them into buying products. For example, there is a common marketing technique called "decoy pricing", which, in a nutshell, involves overpricing one item to make everything else in a store look cheaper. So, when falling victim to this technique, consumers often feel smart for buying the cheaper products when, in fact, they were what the store wanted them to buy in the first place. Interesting, wouldn't you say? The overpriced product was just there to make everything else look cheap, and humans often fall for this simple trick. After all, as we've said, a human's comparison feature is often narrow and hollow, and marketers are well aware of the fact.

A SUMMARY OF THE RATIONALE OF CHAPTERS 16 & 17

And now let's summarise the rationale step by step:
1. The reality is that humans are animals with all kinds of instincts, thoughts and desires — including those that are forbidden.
2. Humans create Rigid Rules and judge others who have what they consider dark thoughts and desires.
3. Humans judge themselves, too.
4. Naturally, to comply with all their rules (which prevent them from being themselves), humans avoid their instincts and dark

thoughts. To do that, they repress forbidden thoughts and desires.

5. So, humans try to keep busy by looking outwards (to avoid encountering their self-created Dragons).

6. Not surprisingly, humans never fix anything (Hidden Associations, Holy Grail, Rigid Rules, etc.), so they continually face the same problems. The more humans ignore issues, the worse they become.

7. To compensate for their self-ignorance, humans rely on comparison to figure out what or where they are. They compete all the time against almost anything.

8. Lastly, humans can't see when they are in a good situation because they ADAPT. Anything can become the new standard. So, even when a human's life is amazing, you can still scare him. He can feel desperate about losing something he doesn't need, even when safe.

Yes, every human has internal surveillance — a spy. And, for many unfortunate humans, even though they are oblivious to the fact, their spies inform them that life is a complete nightmare. Humans with Rigid Rules live their entire lives devoid of deep self-reflection.

So, given that humans are practically incapable of observing themselves, we hunters can watch them instead and take advantage. You must spend a lot of time OBSERVING YOUR QUARRY.

As a result, humans are most often slaves of ignorance. And like we mentioned at the beginning of this chapter, in general, most humans believe they rule their minds, but, instead, they resemble clown kings who are too afraid to go to bed without a light on.

CONCLUSIONS

Hunting any animal on Earth requires patience, resilience and a large amount of attention. The hunter must observe his prey for an extended period. Your advantage will stem from preparation, patience and knowing the human you pursue better than he knows himself. Watching humans, and understanding that they struggle to observe themselves, is critical, which is why we dedicated three chapters to the subject.

Four characteristics of the human mind are judgement, Rigid Rules, comparison and adaption. All these characteristics contribute to humans' lack of self-knowledge by preventing them from looking deep within.

By failing to explore their nature, humans are unable to take full control of their minds and bodies and, consequently, become slaves to unknown internal forces.

Now you know the reasons for humans' ignorance, and all the stuff that looked like nonsense explained in previous chapters of this book is their inability and unwillingness to reflect on and self-investigate their minds.

Yes, humans are kings who don't know their Castles, and if you understand them better than they do, you can manipulate them as you please. How easy can it get?

Before we finish, it is worth mentioning a few more things about the human animal; after all, a few have, indeed, tried to look within, but most often this attempt fails. Why? Let's see ....

BONUS
STIGMA ON EARTH
Another reason for human ignorance

If you have already visited Earth, you will have noticed that some humans step beyond outward looking and partake in activities that allow their thoughts to wander — meditation or yoga for example.

There is no reason to worry, though. Humans almost never have the 'instruction manual' for their minds. So, even when reflecting, they are rarely equipped for all the topics in this book. In other words, humans hardly ever ask their Crew why it reacts a certain way, reflect on their emotions or question their Hidden Associations. The human species almost never does these things.

As mentioned, some humans try meditation. And, yes, the focus of this practice is awareness of sensations and emotions and spending time on one's self. So, in a way, it helps them. However, again, even they don't usually have access to the information contained in this book. These humans do, indeed, look inwards, but without understanding the necessary theory. For example, they barely realise that they have alternative meanings and categories in their minds — a different reality — to those around them. And the few who do almost never understand this fact entirely.

A common philosophy for those who meditate seems to be *"stop craving things, let go and observe."* Yes, meditation is good for humans and helps them gain awareness. However, it doesn't provide all the pieces to the puzzle by, for example, explaining human cravings — the meanings behind them.

Finally, as you can probably imagine, the philosophy of ceasing to crave stuff and letting go far from resonates with Earth's leaders and, therefore, isn't in line with what most humans consider to be for 'winners'.

So, some humans have indeed tried to look inside. However, almost none hold all the pieces (theory, outsider's perspective and time to reflect) required to know themselves. Very few reflect and question their thoughts, and even those who do usually don't have access to the theory.

<u>Wait! What about a thing called psychotherapy?</u>
Isn't this treatment about looking inwards, investigating oneself? Yes, we believe so. However, in our experience, psychotherapy is mostly viewed as a tool restricted to treating conditions such as depression, anxiety, obsessive-compulsive disorders, addictions or low self-esteem. It is rarely used for inner investigation of ordinary humans with no apparent problems. Not often will you see 'winners' (successful and wealthy entrepreneurs, for example), who are NOT facing a crisis, seek psychotherapy to enhance their lives.

In other words, psychotherapy is rarely used as a tool for those brave enough to face their Dragons. No, instead, almost always it's used only to help the weak, the flawed.

<u>A curiosity: The ineffective marketing strategy that you can exploit</u>
On Earth, the world's great brands sell products by using simple, yet powerful, messages that depict winners. Consumer psychologists and marketers know how to appeal to humans and play with their desires. These brands recognise that much of any product's appeal is psychological, and they know what makes their target market 'tick' in order to achieve sales.

Meanwhile, psychologists have a great product and, yet, even society's winners, the highly educated, are usually emotionally illiterate. Why is this?

In our view, the problem starts with terrible marketing of which, most often, portrays psychotherapy as a treatment for issues of self-esteem or mental diseases, not to enhance one's life. The strategy rarely plays with humans' desires and vanity, almost never adequately explains the benefits (beyond being a cure for mental illness) of the treatment and hardly ever uses great leaders to gain trust through, what the marketers call, "celebrity endorsements". Instead, psychotherapy is often linked to humans in need of help.

To give you an idea, some professionals of the mind say that girls envy their brothers' penises, or that boys lust after their mothers. Yikes! Whether true or not, such information has next to no chance of getting 'bums on psychotherapists' seats'.

On the other hand, others try to oversimplify the problem which also doesn't help improve their already low credibility. With an already tainted image, these guys claim that they can provide self-knowledge in 16 sessions (to fit with patients' health plans), which sounds great, don't you think? We wonder if they also throw in a set of steak knives? It's like changing a human's life-long patterns is as easy as delivering a pizza. It should be easy to understand why such an approach fails to appeal to sceptical leaders who don't even know that they have challenges to deal with in the first place.

Regardless of the method, no one praises wisdom and self-knowledge, or plays with humans' vanity and desires to become more powerful, by better understanding themselves. We have never seen therapy promoted as an *"investigative tool for those brave enough to face their inner darkness"*, for example. It is not sold like that. There's a lot of stigma around psychotherapy and, consequently, most humans believe it offers little help for winners.

So, rather than studying how their minds work, the majority of humans favour topics like languages, mathematics, biology, engineering and business. As a result, even the most educated and successful humans often don't possess the basic knowledge we share in this book. And we are only scratching the surface regarding the mechanics of the human mind. Humans are far more complex than you can imagine.

What would happen if Earth's greatest brands adopted the same marketing approach as the psychologists? One thing's for sure: You wouldn't see humans wearing Nike shoes or driving Audi motorcars.

It's true that recently things have started to change, but it will take a long while before humanity reaps any real rewards. Most humans never reflect on discussions about self-knowledge and wisdom. Such talk doesn't affect them.

For example, it should be easy to understand that it is in one's best interests to need less (to escape Survival Mode). However, humans have heard this sentiment countless times, usually from losers, with this rationale: *"I can't be rich, so I tell people that I don't want to be rich,"* which means *"I disdain money, not because I don't want it, but because I can't have it."* These humans also usually say, *"You should need less."* As a result, many humans associate such a view with losers.

Unfortunately for humans (fortunately for us), hardly any of them, even world leaders, have many of the pieces required to solve the puzzle that is the human mind. So, don't worry; we hunters have many years ahead of which to enjoy manipulating our prey. Anyway, for now, this is just a curiosity to help you better understand the situation on Earth.

<u>Note:</u> Funnily enough, if you repeat what we say above about the terrible marketing strategy to other humans, bearing in mind the broken communication system (and the Drawers), they will probably think that we have something against psychotherapists, that we don't think they do a good job, etc., which is not what we're saying. We're just criticising their marketing strategies, not them. Haha!

THE DIFFICULT TASK OF KNOWING ONESELF

Even if humans had all the answers and spent time for self-observation, they would still struggle. Why? Because it is all so f #*!@# difficult and takes hundreds, even thousands, of hours of reflection. Much solitude embedded with reflection is required to forge a human's character. So, because these things are out of question for most humans, they live with the wrong idea of who they are and what they want. Often, who humans think they are is merely a reflection of what their tribe wants them to be.

As a result, humans are haunted by internal Dragons. And to 'kill the beasts', they would first have to face them, spend time with and pay attention to them. Humans would need to check when their brain identifies a threat (when they feel vulnerable, nervous, angry, etc.), notice their own words and pay attention to — and question — when their brain rewards them with pleasure for doing something it believes is right. In other words, they would have to go beyond learning the lessons here. They would have to EXPERIENCE them. After all, humans only really learn from experience. Otherwise, all we have said here would be just words and soon be forgotten.

As years pass by, and desires become more repressed, rediscovering themselves becomes increasingly costly and difficult. To find his real self, a human would have to accept he has been walking the wrong path for many years. And, if you remember the Drawers, you'll know that such a conclusion (that he is wrong) is for losers. So, humans generally take the Weak Captain's approach of denial to create a more palatable reality. Consequently, humans are usually just diluted, warped versions of what they could become if they took control of their kingdoms.

So, as you can see, humans need lots of Resources, Alliances and Trust in the Captain to be fulfilled and to stay out of Survival Mode. They also need TIME to reflect and organise their minds — time that humans hardly have.

In reality, true freedom and self-knowledge require deep introspection and psychological experimentation. Each human must test his ways of living to see what does or doesn't work. But, don't worry, as already explained, humans usually spend their free time looking outwards. And, those who do look inside, lack the tools and outsider's perspective to fix problems they discover.

Now, you are ready to meet the Superiors. Welcome to the final part of this book.

PART VI
SUPERIORS

18

HUNTING GUIDE
KEY NOTES

Believe it or not, you now know more about humans than they do — at least, the vast majority of them. Sure, many say that they understand a bit about how their minds work. The truth, though, is that their knowledge is shallow. It's like recognising the Hierarchy of Needs theory without understanding Hidden Associations. We haven't yet found a prey who grasps every characteristic explained in this book. And one must understand them ALL (and spend a great deal of time in reflection) when hunting humans.

Regardless of whether or not humans realise, deep within their minds, each pursues a Holy Grail, sometimes more than one. While doing so, they continually monitor their minimum requirements to feel safe — all from inside the Captain's Cabin. And, by the time the Captain receives the information, it has been filtered by Hidden Association and Drawers and guided by Expanded Self-Interest, which translates into feelings, emotions and desires.

Let's summarise the human characteristics. Keep this summary close at hand; you'll find it useful during your hunt.

ISOLATED & WITH AN ALTERNATIVE REALITY

1. Just codes:

Human don't express themselves as clearly as they think — their internal system is highly inefficient. So, they often confuse their communication system with some sort of telepathy. At the same time, humans have no idea about how much their words reveal — like when they criticise something. Pay attention to what your prey talks about; you will gain invaluable insight into what he pays attention to, how he perceives it (his inner reality) and how you can manipulate him.

2. Each human's reality is unique:

Inside the brain:

Every human is like a captain controlling a ship from inside his cabin (isolated dark room). The Messenger translates everything that reaches the Captain. Everything. And, humans confuse information the Messenger supplies with reality. They, in effect, 'see' the world with their brains, not eyes. So, humans project reality (hallucinate), and what they believe to be real is highly influenced by Hidden Associations and Drawers.

Hidden Associations:

"What does it mean to this animal? Can it differentiate between assumptions and facts?" Humans are unaware of the meanings in their minds, so they have a neurological tendency towards delusion and are haunted by associations of which they are unaware.

Extremes:

"How does this animal categorise the situation? Does it have a few Drawers or more?" Most often, humans don't have a clue about the categories in their minds and how the Messenger separates information into Drawers, which leads to extreme conclusions and reactions. Most often, humans are stuck between 100% right or wrong, 100% winner or Loser, etc., and, for them, this creates perceived threats.

<u>Defence mechanisms:</u>
The Messenger will usually try to preserve the Captain and status quo. So, given humans' Rigid Rules and the extremes caused by a small number of Drawers, the Weak Captain's defence of blame and denial (to create alternative realities) comes into play far more often than it should. To cope with life, humans also repress a large part of reality. In other words, they have an in-built fake-news generator to protect the Weak Captain.

<u>Repetition:</u>
One consequence of all of the above is Repetition, of which humans are condemned. You see, humans are usually responsible for their recurring problems. The ongoing issues humans face are usually determined by what they pay attention to (or are able to notice), desire, and how they behave.

Finally, never forget:

<u>The timings of the Crew and Captain are different:</u>
Unlike at the Captain level, it takes a long time to change the Crew (specifically the Messenger). So, even if the Captain understands this book's concepts, he still must slowly explain each of them to his Crew, which is strongly influenced by past experiences and not easy to convince. It takes lots of practice. Therefore, even when a human understands the concepts, for a while, his Messenger (with its same Hidden Associations separated into big Drawers and the same conflicting Holy Grail, etc.) will continue to send the wrong message. In the short-term, all a human can do is be aware that the messages he receives might be skewed, and so he must question them. Doing this takes a lot of effort.

THE TRANSLATOR
IN BETWEEN REALTIES & DESIRES

<u>3. Emotions & desires:</u>
Emotions and desires play a crucial role in human behaviour. They tell a human what his brain wants, and because they seem so real, humans

rarely question them and, consequently, become obedient puppets of an ancient central system designed for the jungle. Let's not forget that the brain isn't always right.

<u>4. Humans' lack of an outsider's point of view:</u>
Thanks to their inability to look at themselves objectively, it's almost impossible for humans to realise that they should question their emotions, desires and reality. Consequently, like a marionette, humans spend their lives oblivious to the strings that guide them.

WHAT DRIVES THE ANIMAL — FEAR & VANITY ALL GUIDED BY EXPANDED SELF-INTEREST

<u>5. Expanded Self-Interest:</u>
"What's in it for my prey? Can it see the long-term?" Humans' ignorance about rewards is enormous. So, they most often live in a fairy tale and believe in actions for no return. As a hunter, you must consider ALL rewards that humans seek, not just those relating to money and recognition. You must take into account their pursuit of maximum pleasure and minimum pain and also whether they can consider the long-term — their ability to look ahead will determine how they judge what is good or bad for them.

<u>6. Fear & related feelings:</u>
The sense of vulnerability manifests itself in more than fear. It can take many forms, such as anger, nervousness, hatred, anxiety, stress and even aggression. *"What is my prey's minimum level to feel safe? Is my prey above or below it?"* Most humans behave like cornered and starving animals because they are permanently below the minimum levels of Alliances (social recognition and acceptance), Resources (money and health) or Trust in the Captain (self-esteem) to feel safe. They are in Survival Mode either because they really do need more Alliances or Resources (like in the case of a starving animal), or because they confuse needs with wants and, therefore, raise the bar artificially to need something at a higher level and then become desperate to get it. It is usually easy to infuriate your prey when it's in Survival Mode because it is barely rationale. As a hunter, avoid humans who are beyond the

minimum levels to feel safe; they are difficult to manipulate. Choose an easier, more desperate target.

<u>7. Vanity, pride & admiration:</u>
"What is this creature's definition of success? What is it proud of? What is its Holy Grail?" Knowing a human's Holy Grail will enable you to be a few steps ahead. After all, the rule is simple: When a human moves closer to his Holy Grail he feels good; if he slips farther away he feels bad. Generally, humans' Holy Grails are unclear for their Captains, which is strange considering how much they influence humans' decisions.

NO TIME, CHANCE OR EVEN WILLINGNESS FOR REFLECTION

<u>8. Rigid Rules:</u>
Humans create internal rules to live in society. Often, though, these rules ignore human nature and are overly rigid, which makes them impossible to obey. And because their 'guides for life' are so uncompromising, humans are only allowed a narrow set of thoughts, behaviours, attitudes — even aspirations — and so they spend life unable to access their inner unsettling truths — Dragons that haunt them for life.

<u>9. Time to observe:</u>
"Has my prey ever explored its Dungeons?" Humans unknowingly spend their lives denying their thoughts and desires. They think they succeed in feeling nothing, but their emotions and desires are there anyway, and so humans end up being at the behest of forces they ignore.

By not paying attention to themselves, and so failing to feel anything, humans forgo the tools for understanding what affects them and why; they are condemned to self-ignorance.

As a result, most often, humans' lives resemble an internal 'to-do list' with meaningless outward-looking hobbies that do little for self-understanding. Unable to access their inner truths, and burdened by self-ignorance, most humans compare and compete excessively to gauge their worth; they can't assess their real situation. The consequences feature on pretty much every page of this book.

As mentioned at the beginning of this book, only a few of these human characteristics are unknown to most humans. For example, if you bring up Repetition, most would say, *"Yes, people usually make the same mistakes again and again. It's kind of a continuous cycle."* And, they think they understand. However, their analysis is shallow — far more so than what we are talking about.

Before we finish, here is another way to see parts of what we have discussed in this book:

THE LAYER WHERE THE CAPTAIN EXISTS
Squeezed by the Crew

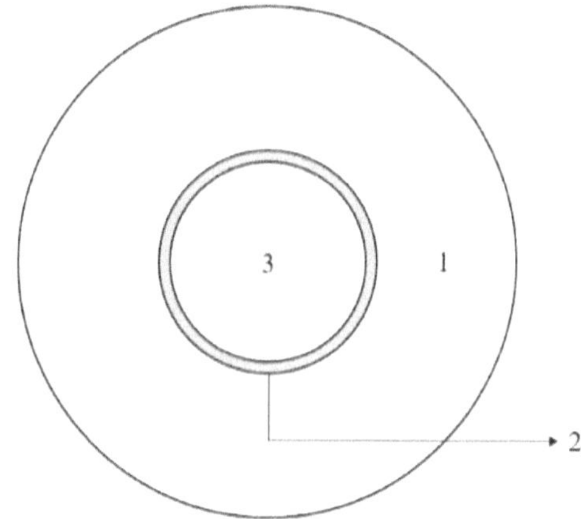

1 - Crew – *Filters reality that is captured through senses such as eyes and ears.*
- Decides the fraction of information to send
- Edits information using Hidden Association and Drawers
- Uses blame and denial whenever necessary

2 - Captain (thin grey circle) – *Makes a small amount of the decisions and thinks he is in control.*

3 - Crew – *Sends emotions and desires back to the Captain while always focused on escaping fear and chasing vanity.*
- Manages:
    - Organs (heartbeat, body temperature, etc.)
    - Emotions and desires
    - Repressed memories
    - Holy Grail (s)
    - Rigid Rules
    - Levels of minimum requirements
    - Expanded Self-Interest

The Crew judges whether or not the animal is in Survival Mode, getting farther away from or closer to its Holy Grail.

Figure 4: The thin layer where the Captain exists.

Lastly, don't forget that humans are complicated, so it usually takes several years for a hunter to comprehend fully and apply the teachings of this book. Mastering the ways of human beings takes practice, but it's worth the effort.

Let's now, finally, meet the Superiors, creatures like no other.

19
THE SUPERIORS
PILOTING THE ANIMAL

Superiors are scarce, enhanced human beings. Although they look like and can interbreed with regular humans, the distance between Superiors and regular humans is greater than that between a human and a chimpanzee. As a hunter, you must avoid Superiors. You will never trick and manipulate them; they will mess you up.

Superiors understand the concepts in this book. They are wise kings in their Castles — they certainly don't fear Dungeons. You could compare Superiors to seasoned spacecraft pilots. You see, they recognise that they are *piloting* an animal, and they do it pretty well.

How does an ordinary human being become a Superior? Well, he must first be willing to place the characteristics of a Superior in his Holy Grail, learn everything discussed in this book and practice. A lot.

Let's look at the characteristics of Superiors.

BECOMING A DOT
The great divorce

To become a Superior, a human must undergo an internal separation — a divorce between his Captain and Crew. He must split the parts of himself that he can control from the rest, which he can only train (or tame). By doing so, a human becomes a mere dot inside his head, and he pilots his body like a spaceship.

This separation doesn't require forgoing feelings, becoming a psychopath. Instead, a Superior recognises that he and what he feels are not the same. Emotions are indicators, not absolute truths. So, a Superior pays attention to and questions his feelings as if monitoring a control panel, and he reacts in a manner that he believes appropriate, not how his Crew wants. Sensations are advisors, not bosses. This divorce between Captain and Crew allows Superiors to see the world through the lens of Expanded Self-Interest and better understand themselves and others. Post separation, a human grows his rational self and defines who he is as an individual.

LIFE AS A PERMANENT OUTSIDER

Superiors are able to view their lives from an outsider's perspective, just like regular humans have no problem challenging foreign rituals, cultures and behaviours. Superiors can question aspects of human life because they are able to observe from the outside. They examine their emotions, sensations, Hidden Association, Drawers — their entire reality. By becoming a dot within their heads, a Superior achieves masterful control of his body and mind.

BROADER RULES
A requirement for exploration

Superiors know that they pilot an animal with instincts — a creature with dark thoughts and desires. So, to explore their minds, they destroy established internal rules for acceptance and behaviour and develop their OWN, which are broad. Slowly, they create independent rules and defer matters of judgement to their conscience, not the Rigid Rules of others. Consequently, they are able to explore their minds and Dungeons, unafraid of meeting Dragons.

Superiors explore their Dungeons, question their Hidden Associations and are prepared to face what they find. *"Why do I compete with this human? Why do I hate him? Why do I love that frustrating human?"* Things like that.

OBSERVE THE QUARRY

To reach the rarefied state of a Superior takes time, and humans must put in the 'hard yards' to observe themselves.

Superiors understand that the two key words in the line by Sun Tzu *"Know the enemy and know yourself; in a hundred battles you will never be in peril,"* are *"know yourself".* This knowledge is essential for completeness. **Superiors realise that the prey they must observe is, actually, themselves.** By exploring their thoughts and emotions, Superiors escape haunting memories and are free to chase the future.

HIDDEN ASSOCIATIONS & DRAWERS
The Permanent Investigation

As explained earlier, Superiors use their emotions to their advantage. They see being irritated as an opportunity to understand better how their minds work, the meaning behind the irritation, and, when necessary, they try to change the meaning interpreted by their Crew. Superiors know that as they gain self-awareness and discover what they want, it makes less sense to become upset by external things that are not real threats. By paying attention to, and destroying wrong Hidden Associations, Superiors slowly break the pattern of angriness commonly seen in humans. Consequently, they hardly ever get annoyed at others; Superiors are secure and robust.

Superiors are NOT Brain Puppets. Instead, they 'turn the tables' and teach their brains how to react. Superiors are masters of their emotions.

Because their minds have an almost infinite number of Drawers, Superiors are unafraid of self-exploration. They know life isn't black and white, and so they don't swing from one extreme to another — 100% right or wrong, winner or loser. No fake threat or small mistake will send a Superior to the Loser Drawer.

LOW MINIMUM REQUIREMENTS

Superiors understand reality better than regular humans, thanks to their countless Drawers. They know that to manage minimum requirements, PERCEPTION is essential and they understand that a high need for Resources or Alliances is a weakness. Therefore, Superiors break their Hidden Associations, adjust their internal rules and are almost permanently beyond Survival Mode. Superiors NEED little and WANT big. They are free.

THE SUPERIOR'S HOLY GRAIL

Superiors don't have to live in poverty to need little. Having low minimum requirements is a mindset, not a bank balance, and Superiors are, actually, often wealthy. Despite having low minimum requirements, these superhumans still search for the impossible without needing to achieve it.

For a human to become a Superior, he must dedicate himself to introspection and self-development. Also, rather than adopt a pre-packaged super-self courtesy of his social group, a human must create his own with a clear definition of success in mind.

Superiors understand the complexities of life and, so, don't define success by single events. The dream of becoming a Superior is but one of many elements that make up their tailor-made Holy Grails.

SOME CONSEQUENCES

<u>Low minimum requirements and a unique, well-balanced Holy Grail applied</u>
Take this book as an example. Obviously, we, the authors, want it to be successful, so it's part of our collective Holy Grail. Without a doubt, some critics will say the book is rubbish, and their negative views will make us feel farther away from our Holy Grail. However, with a well-defined and balanced Holy Grail (that, by the way, should not be based on a single project like a book), and an understanding of the book's merits, we, as Superiors, are not threatened by setbacks or criticisms. We don't deny critics. Instead, we listen and learn. Hey, there's always room for improvements! Do you see? Criticism is necessary — essential for growth.

At the same time, should this book become a best-seller, we won't bathe in the bliss of euphoria. This book is but a small part of our Holy Grail. Can you see how stable and almost unbreakable Superiors are?

Less comparison & competition

Superiors have high levels of self-knowledge because they continually explore their minds. As a consequence, to determine who they are, they don't compare themselves with others. Superiors don't need many Alliances, either; a little social acceptance among close family and friends is usually enough. As explained, having their own rules of acceptance and behaviour, Superiors defer matters of judgement to their conscience.

While many humans compete excessively to prove their worth, Superiors recognise that competitive behaviour is more appropriate for male baboons wishing to win over a mate than for humans. In modern society, a human can get a partner and money, etc., without being excessively competitive.

Superiors needn't win battles to build Trust in the Captain because it's already there due to their deep understanding of their abilities, skills, needs and goals. They can compete from time to time, for fun or necessity, but not nearly as often as regular humans. A Superior understands that the real battle is with one's self.

An interesting & permanent investigation

Superiors understand that self-investigation never ends. It can't. Like an elite athlete who ceases to train will turn to flab, a Superior who stops looking inward will mess up his mind.

At the beginning, self-investigation is extremely difficult (especially while rules of acceptance are still rigid). Over time, though, if done right, it becomes fascinating.

With relaxed rules of acceptance, Superiors live in a Zen-like state. They enjoy self-exploration. And, due to the multitude of Hidden Associations humans face every day, it is an endless pursuit, which is the best part.

From birth to death – seeing the big picture

Regular humans distance themselves from the fact that they are animals, creatures that eventually perish. Superiors, on the other hand, use their mortality to their advantage. Doing so provides them with a realistic perspective on life; they see the futility of comparing themselves with others.

Superiors plan for the long-term while aware that no human's lifespan is certain. After all, at any time, every human is one lousy diagnosis or distracted driver away from oblivion. Though they understand that overthinking death can be troubling, at the same time, Superiors know not thinking about it is denial. So, holding death close helps Superiors to choose which battles to fight and, therefore, make wise decisions.

Mindfulness of their mortality combined with deep introspection enables Superiors to create ideal Holy Grails, and so everything they admire points in the right direction. Appreciation of life's uncertainties helps Superiors value their lives and the lives of others.

Kicking the pleasure drug

Finally, regular humans are generally addicted to pleasure. They are what we call "pleasure junkies", consumed by an insatiable thirst for a new thrill.

Regardless of the goal, once achieved, most humans soon NEED more — more money, more wins, more friends. Pleasure junkies' lack of self-knowledge drives them on a continuous search for signs that they are worthwhile human beings, that they are socially accepted.

The endless need for thrills haunts most humans. And, when dealing with such desperate creatures, hunting becomes easy.

In contrast, a Superior's definition of happiness is inner peace, not strong feelings. Excitement and happiness are not one and the same. It's true that Superiors do all they can to be happy; however, they appreciate that happiness is pure and if one is unaware of its presence, not easily felt. On the other hand, regular humans often notice happiness only when it's gone, and so their pursuit is never-ending.

The experienced rider

In our view, regular humans (specifically their Captains) control their bodies and minds like cowboys in a rodeo — they attempt to stay mounted while the bull does its utmost to throw them into the dirt. Control is minimal. Remember, humans are, in essence, animals. With time and training, however, Superiors learn to ride and dominate the bucking bull.

CONCLUSIONS

Superiors are masters of their minds — superbeings. They are complete and have low needs and well-defined Holy Grails. Every Superior knows which prey each human should observe.

Finally, hunters, avoid Superiors — they will mess you up. Humans, try to be one.

The End

FINAL WORDS

COUNTER-ATTACK

Some will view my writing *The Art of Hunting Humans* as akin to crossing the Rubicon — a villainous act of no return that will brand me an eternal enemy of humanity. As you digest the closing pages, though, I hope you realise that this book is not a guide for hunting humans; rather, it is my quirky explanation for why humans behave in the ways that they do and how their minds work.

I wrote this book from the point of view of an outsider — a visitor from another world — which I believe was necessary to expose human characteristics and the problems we all face.

No author is an island, and my influences comprise a broad range of theories, philosophies and books — no, not all books are for losers! Many are great, but I needed to get your attention. Psychoanalysis and psychotherapies, such as cognitive behavioural therapy, have impacted me — so too has neuroscience. I also get inspiration from philosophers and business strategies, such as Blue Ocean Strategy. Change management principles, and sales and marketing techniques, have also impacted me.

I must state clearly that I am not a psychologist, nor a professional writer. My background is in engineering and finance, which may, in part, explain my sceptical life view. Above all, please note that this book is a work of fiction.

The concepts in this book are simplistic and are my interpretations of several books and theories. Of course, humans are far more complex than the framework I suggest. However, I believe a simple approach is necessary — a tome the size of *War and Peace* couldn't do justice to the topic of Hidden Associations alone. So, I offer just a glimpse. Some kind of 'rustic wisdom', let's say.

Simplicity, though, doesn't make the concepts easy to understand and apply. To master them, many hours are required. After all, it's one thing to convince the Captain, but getting the Crew on board is something else altogether.

So, I am well aware that this book isn't for everyone. Just a few. Let's face it, most people want simple solutions for complex problems. And, so for them, a guide that espouses positive thinking and correct posture (known as "power positions") would probably be more appropriate. The problem, though, is that those books and techniques don't come close to addressing the problems humanity grapples with.

I also make some harsh criticisms and express several controversial opinions. Do I want to stir hate? No, not at all. Those who truly understand my concepts will know that is far from the case.

My purpose is to raise attention to the importance of self-reflection and the pursuit of wisdom. These things are often undervalued in society due to, in my view, poor marketing by the psychology fraternity, which, consequently, stigmatises those who pursue inner knowledge or attend therapy.

I want to get people talking, regardless of whether or not they agree with me, so I've tried to be as controversial as possible. Accepting or rejecting my simplistic explanations of the human mind is less important to me than getting people to recognise the need for self-reflection focused on self-knowledge and wisdom.

I call those who have mastered my concepts "Superiors", which may seem provocative and arrogant. I'm just trying to tease you and counter-attack centuries of humanity undervaluing the pursuit of wisdom and self-knowledge. Call these wise humans what you will.

While at first, the general message of this book appears to be that humans are weak and you must explore and exploit their ignorance and flaws, you probably now know that isn't the message. Given you have completed this book, I hope it's clear that I have tried to explain the advantages of being more aware of our perceptions, beliefs, Hidden Associations, Drawers, Holy Grails and minimum requirements, and not spending our lives led by invisible forces. That's the real message. I wanted to create a sense of urgency for change, highlight the importance of self-knowledge and wisdom, and expose problems with the status quo.

The truth is that to change anything, we first must confront reality by exposing the problems humans face and articulating a convincing argument for change. So, that's why I expose what, in my view, are human flaws and explain how to explore them.

I believe it's time for humans to escape Survival Mode and be proud of trying to know themselves. They need the tools, and they also need to admire others who pursue self-knowledge. It's time to fix vanity.

Last but not least, my first child will soon be born, and this book is for him. I want to make sure my child understands humans — just in case I'm not around as a guide. I don't want to leave things to chance.

If you liked this book:
- *Sign up at HuntingHumans.com to keep in contact and receive updates from us.*
- *Follow us on Facebook, Instagram, and Twitter.*
- *Take your time to leave a review with your favourite retailer.*

HuntingHumans.com

#wannabewise

Thank you